New Approaches to Management

Creating Practical Systems
of Management Information
and Management by Objectives

J. Victor Baldridge
Michael L. Tierney

New Approaches to Management

 Jossey-Bass Publishers
San Francisco • Washington • London • 1979

NEW APPROACHES TO MANAGEMENT
Creating Practical Systems of Management Information and Management by Objectives
by J. Victor Baldridge and Michael L. Tierney

Copyright © 1979 by: Jossey-Bass, Inc., Publishers
433 California Street
San Francisco, California 94104
&
Jossey-Bass Limited
28 Banner Street
London EC1Y 8QE

Library of Congress Cataloging in Publication Data

Baldridge, J. Victor
    New approaches to management

    (The Jossey-Bass series in higher education)
    Bibliography: p.
    Includes index.
    1. Universities and colleges—Administration—Decision making—Data
processing. I. Tierney, Michael L., 1950–   joint author. II. Title.
LB2341.B268   378.73   79–88105
ISBN 0-87589-420-8

Manufactured in the United States of America

JACKET DESIGN BY WILLI BAUM

FIRST EDITION

Code 7926

The Jossey-Bass Series
in Higher Education

A Publication of the
Higher Education Research Institute

Preface

This book is addressed to college and university administrators at all levels, but it should be particularly useful to anyone interested in or involved in using computerized data for decision making within any academic institution. Its purpose is to examine the value of *management information systems* (MIS) and *management by objectives* (MBO)—two innovative approaches that colleges and universities have begun to use widely.

We concentrate on institutions that received grants from a foundation to implement these innovations, but our goal is much broader than a foundation report. We seek to answer the general question of whether these new managerial techniques really help improve organizational processes. From our experiences with the institutions in this study, we have learned much about how to implement management innovations—and how not to do so. We believe that the insights we have gained have implications for all kinds of colleges and universities. Thus, this book deals not only with the narrow question of whether these particular colleges—many of them small liberal arts institutions —made improvements but also with the issue of whether such managerial innovations can help a broad spectrum of colleges and universities. Our conclusion is that the efforts of these institutions can be informative for most of higher education.

Research Procedures

In 1974 the Exxon Education Foundation asked the Higher Education Research Institute (HERI) in Los Angeles to study the impact of Exxon's Resource Allocation Management Program (RAMP) on the forty-nine institutions receiving grants under the program. Even though new techniques for improving management practices in higher education had gained widespread attention in the previous few years, little was actually known about how a college's educational effectiveness is affected by its management procedures. On a more fundamental level, it was important to determine whether improvements in management techniques really do have a measurable impact on an institution. Thus, the principal purpose of our study was to determine whether, and how, colleges are affected by changes in their management techniques.

In our evaluation of the RAMP projects, we examined a variety of areas where impact was possible: administrative behavior, morale and general atmosphere of the college, planning and budgeting activities, and financial stability. We concentrated on the behavioral consequences of management changes for administrators, faculty, staff, and students as measured by:

1. The behavior of administrative officers before, during, and after the implementation of these new management practices.
2. The behavior of faculty members, particularly those with administrative responsibilities, before, during, and after implementation.
3. An analysis of these data to determine (a) which behavioral patterns inhibit and which reinforce the implementation of sound management procedures; (b) which behavioral characteristics are modified by new management procedures and which resist modification; and (c) the extent to which the

institution's management practices affect its educational achievements with its students.

To carry out these analyses, our research was both comparative, to examine the differences between institutions, and longitudinal, to determine changes over time. We think a comparative framework is the best approach for research on institutions. It is difficult to tell whether a new management technique had much influence on one institution without a comparison of its impact on other institutions. All but five of the RAMP project institutions were private liberal arts colleges enrolling fewer than 5,000 students. By looking at these institutions under a variety of conditions, we were able to make useful comparisons which help put our findings in perspective. We constantly tried to contrast experiences on one campus with those on another, so that lessons could be learned about implementing new management techniques in a variety of circumstances.

Because our research design was also longitudinal, we wanted to collect data from each institution *before* any work was done on its RAMP project, *during* project implementation, and *after* implementation. Within the constraints of existing staff and resources, we were able to collect data on each campus as soon as possible after receiving notification from the Exxon Education Foundation that a RAMP award had been made; but many grant recipients had already implemented major parts of their projects even before they received their grants. At the other extreme, some institutions were not able to implement their projects before the five years of our evaluation were up. Thus, a major concern in our repeated data collection was to determine the state of implementation of each project. This problem of timing imposed certain limits on our analyses, as will be evident in Chapter One, but it did not pose insurmountable difficulties.

This complex research design was supported by a multifaceted data base that included interviews, questionnaires, information from other studies, and in-depth case studies. We visited every campus several times, conducting scores of interviews at each location with key administrators, faculty members, and student leaders. People most closely associated with the RAMP project received the most attention, but we also interviewed people who were not directly associated with the project. These interviews provided a rich source of subjective and impressionistic data about the project and its impact.

We also administered a battery of questionnaires to key administrators, faculty members, and students on every campus and then repeated this battery following completion of the project. Among the questions that we asked approximately a dozen top administrators in each institution, two seemed particularly important for judging the success of the project: (1) "Has this project become a fundamental part of the college management process, or is it used on an ad hoc basis, or is it not used at all?" (2) "How would you rate the overall success of this project; very successful, moderately successful, disappointing, no opinion?"

Beyond interviews and questionnaires, we also tapped several related sources of data. One such data base was the U.S. Office of Education's Higher Education General Information Survey (HEGIS), which contains data on the level of enrollment, number of faculty positions, and fiscal characteristics of all institutions of higher education in the United States. A second source was the Cooperative Institutional Research Program, an annual survey of entering freshmen, jointly sponsored by the American Council on Education and the University of California at Los Angeles.

Finally, beyond these data, which allowed us to make quantitative comparisons among the RAMP project institutions, we wanted to gather more "in-depth" information on a few institutions to understand how they used different management techniques in different ways and to analyze some of the most successful and least successful projects in great detail. In this "worst/best case" analysis, we focused on five institutions to find out why they were successes: Arkansas College, Clarkson College of Technology (New York), Earlham College (Indiana), Furman University (South Carolina), Wesleyan University (Connecticut). Their projects form the five case studies in Chapters Three and Five. For obvious reasons, the least successful institutions are not mentioned by name in this book, but their problems contributed to its conclusions, particularly in Chapter Eight.

Following our opening chapter, in which we give a general overview of the RAMP projects and some specific conclusions about their impact, we describe the management information systems (Chapter Two) and offer two case studies to illustrate them (Chapter Three). Chapters Four and Five do the same for the management by objectives programs. In Chapters Six and Seven, we examine the impact of both kinds of projects. Some projects seemed to have very little impact; others improved the planning process or had significant influence on financial and budgetary procedures; and still others affected the morale and social environment of the entire campus. Thus, many projects succeeded, while others failed; and in Chapter Eight we analyze the factors that appear to support or undermine such management innovations. There we outline the lessons we have learned from the RAMP evaluation about how to structure, support, and organize management innovations. And in Chapter Nine we conclude with additional findings about cost control in general within higher education, involving both management innovation and other economies.

Acknowledgments

The research for this book was conducted under a grant from the Exxon Education Foundation. Two people at Exxon whose support and insights were greatly appreciated are Walter Kenworthy and Richard Johnson.

The original investigators in this research were Alexander W. Astin and Lewis C. Solmon at the Higher Education Research Institute. Their contributions are, of course, substantial. Michele Harway also provided leadership on the project for three and a half years. C. E. Christian, Maurice Salter, Lewis C. Solmon, and Beverly Watkins conducted interviews. Computer analyses were performed by Gerald Richardson, James Henson, Leonard Woren, and Rita Sherrei. Much credit goes to Barbara Adams for her work on the case studies of Clarkson College, Arkansas College, and Earlham College. And Carole Feldman, Natalie Kohon, Marilyn Downing, and Deborah Trout graciously helped in typing the manuscript.

So many consultants have aided us at various stages of the project that if we tried to mention them all by name we would undoubtedly leave someone out. So we will simply declare our indebtedness to all those whose expertise assisted us along the way.

Our thanks to all of these associates for their help and support.

August 1979

J. Victor Baldridge
Malibu, California

Michael L. Tierney
University Park, Pennsylvania

Contents

        Impact   146

Eight   Implementing Managerial Innovations
        Successfully   165

Nine   Controlling College Costs   192

        References   208

        Index   213

The Authors

J. Victor Baldridge is senior research sociologist at the Higher Education Research Institute in Los Angeles. He also teaches in the higher education program at the University of California, Los Angeles.

Baldridge was awarded the B.A. degree in sociology from Lambuth College (1963) and, from Yale University, the B.D. degree in social ethics (1966), the M.A. degree in sociology (1967), and the Ph.D. degree in sociology (1968). His specialties are administration, organization theory, organizational change processes, and faculty collective bargaining. He was a faculty member at Stanford University (1968–1974) and assistant vice-president for academic affairs at California State University at Fresno (1974–1976). In 1978, *Change* magazine selected him as one of the "100 Young Leaders of the Academy."

Baldridge has published eleven books, including *Power and Conflict in the University* (1971); *Academic Governance* (1971); *Unions on Campus: A National Study of the Conse-*

xviii New Approaches to Management

quences of Faculty Bargaining (with F. R. Kemerer, 1975); and *Policy Making and Effective Leadership: A National Study of Academic Management* (with D. V. Curtis, G. Ecker, and G. L. Riley, 1978). He has written some fifty articles and book chapters on higher education administration and organization theory and has directed numerous research projects dealing with higher education management.

Baldridge and his wife, Patricia L. Miller, live in Malibu, California.

Michael L. Tierney is assistant professor of higher education and research associate of the Center for the Study of Higher Education at Pennsylvania State University.

Tierney was awarded the B.A. degree in history (1972) and the M.A. degree in educational psychology (1973) from the University of California, Santa Barbara, and the Ph.D. degree in education (1977) from the University of California, Los Angeles. Prior to joining Pennsylvania State University, he was employed as research analyst at the Higher Education Research Institute in Los Angeles, working primarily on the Exxon RAMP study.

His current research activities at Pennsylvania State include the study of demographic trends in the Commonwealth of Pennsylvania, student college choice behaviors, and management control systems in colleges and universities.

He has authored and coauthored several articles and chapters in books on academic governance, administrator job satisfaction, and the economic aspects of education in American history. Forthcoming is an ERIC monograph (with K. P. Mortimer) on the management of decline, titled *The Three Rs for the 1980s: Reductions, Reallocations, and Retrenchment.*

Tierney and his wife, Lauren, live in State College, Pennsylvania.

To Patricia and Lauren

New Approaches to Management

Creating Practical Systems
of Management Information
and Management by Objectives

Chapter One

Overview and Major Conclusions

In the early 1970s, colleges and universities in the United States faced a series of crises. Public support had diminished, financial situations had deteriorated, enrollment shortfalls had occurred frequently, and an oversupply of faculty had undermined the academic job market. Private liberal arts colleges were particularly hard hit by these developments. Dozens of small liberal arts colleges closed their doors, and many that remained open were plagued by financial problems, declining enrollments, and intense competition from less expensive public colleges. In order to increase the flow of money to support the private sector, numerous programs of financial support were developed. Help came from foundations and from student aid programs that allowed students to spend money in private institutions; the federal government continued and expanded its programs of capital grants for private colleges; and fund drives were conducted at scores of private colleges in the early and mid 1970s. In addition, private liberal arts colleges, like most other institutions, began to experiment with computerized "management information

systems," "Delphi techniques," "management by objectives,"
and other management improvement strategies. Some of these
programs were specifically designed to affect the financial problems; others were used to improve planning, staffing, and curriculum development.

In 1973, to promote wider use of management improvement strategies, the Exxon Education Foundation embarked on
a program of grants called the Resource Allocation and Management Program (RAMP). The program was limited to private
liberal arts colleges and universities. In material announcing the
program, Exxon asked these colleges and universities to submit proposals that would make changes in their management
practices:

> Generally speaking, the management prac-
> tices implemented should be designed to remove the
> crisis and opportunistic elements from the ways in
> which decisions are made. While the needs of indi-
> vidual colleges will differ, we assume that modern-
> izing management practices will usually include (1)
> a clear redefinition of authority and responsibility
> within the institution, (2) a definition of the objec-
> tives of the institution and its constituent units,
> (3) a system of *continuous comparison of achieve-
> ments to objectives*, (4) a system requiring a review
> of all possible options before any decision is made,
> and (5) a management information system capable
> of projecting the financial, personnel, and physical
> space allocation consequences of each option being
> reviewed.
>
> A project that does not demonstrate changes
> of this type in the decision-making procedures is
> unlikely to be supported. Prediction models, man-
> agement information systems, program-budgeting
> practices, and advanced record-keeping procedures
> are powerful aids in achieving these modifications
> of management behavior, but the project descrip-
> tion must relate these management tools to new
> management practices on the part of the institu-
> tion's officers.

Table 1. Institutions That Received RAMP Grants
and Participated in the Research

Adelphi University (N.Y.)	Mount Saint Mary's College (Calif.)
Alfred University (N.Y.)	Ohio Dominican College (Ohio)
Arkansas College (Ark.)	Oklahoma Baptist University (Okla.)
Augsburg College (Minn.)	Otterbein College (Ohio)
Azusa Pacific College (Calif.)	Pacific Union College (Calif.)
Bishop College (Texas)	Philadelphia College of Textiles
Carleton College (Minn.)	and Science (Pa.)
Carroll College (Wis.)	Rider College (N.J.)
Clarkson College of Technology (N.Y.)	Roanoke College (Va.)
Colby College (Maine)	Roosevelt University (Ill.)
College of Saint Thomas (Minn.)	Rosemont College (Pa.)
College of Wooster (Ohio)	Saint Lawrence University (N.Y.)
Concordia College at Moorhead	Sarah Lawrence College (N.Y.)
(Minn.)	Shaw University (N.C.)
Dartmouth College (N.H.)	Stevens Institute of Technology (N.J.)
Drake University (Iowa)	Union College (N.Y.)
Earlham College (Ind.)	University of Bridgeport (Conn.)
Fisk University (Tenn.)	University of Tulsa (Okla.)
Furman University (S.C.)	Upsala College (N.J.)
Goucher College (Md.)	Wells College (N.Y.)
Gustavus Adolphus College (Minn.)	Wesleyan University (Conn.)
Haverford College (Pa.)	Westminster College (Utah)
Howard University (Wash., D.C.)	West Virginia Wesleyan College (W.V.)
Illinois Wesleyan University (Ill.)	Wiley College (Texas)
Lone Mountain College (Calif.)	Worcester Polytechnic Institute (Mass.)
Marquette University (Wis.)	

Approximately two hundred institutions applied for grants under the Exxon program. The forty-nine institutions listed in Table 1 eventually received grants, in groups funded over the next several years.

The Exxon Foundation supported a wide variety of management development projects at these institutions. It was concerned that no one model should dominate the program and that a spectrum of management improvement strategies should be tested. As a result, no two projects were alike, although two major types of activity predominated: (1) the gathering and computerization of data through "management information systems" (MIS) and (2) the improved use of data in planning through "management by objectives" (MBO) systems.

Among the forty-nine institutions, the development of management information systems was the most frequent project goal. Many institutions simply needed to clean up and standardize their data base on student records, financial accounts, personnel and alumni records, and physical plant inventories. In most cases, the problem was to standardize the data system throughout the institution and make it compatible with national data systems, such as the Higher Education General Information Survey maintained by the U.S. Office of Education. Computers are now used extensively for building institutional data banks, but some colleges had virtually no data bases and started their computerized MIS data bank from scratch. They wanted to be able to analyze data on their operations—such as the relation between program costs and program enrollment—more carefully, if not for the first time. Several other colleges, however, had already developed large, sophisticated data banks and had used them for years. Their goal, through their RAMP project, was not merely to collect data, maintain them in usable order, and analyze them, but instead to develop computer simulation models that would allow them to predict future trends or show the likely future impact of current decisions. These few institutions developed "advanced" management information systems with sophisticated computer software. By putting various assumptions about the future into their computer programs, they could simulate the possible enrollment or financial impact of different decisions for five, ten, or more years into the future.

The other institutions also made use of data-bank or advanced MIS strategies but developed "management by objectives" (MBO) as their primary focus. Approximately one third of all the RAMP projects involved an MBO approach. Rather than concentrating only on data collection or computer simulation, it involves improved use of data in goal setting and planning. Thus, administrators at several of the institutions argued that they could not use their MIS data well unless they had management programs to increase the sophistication of divisional and department administrators. Their RAMP projects concentrated on training managers in each department of the institution to use data, set goals, and undertake data- and goal-based planning, instead of focusing on more elaborate analytical and simulation procedures.

During our assessment of Exxon's program, people repeatedly asked us the same question: Are management innovations really of value? That is, are their benefits really worth their costs? To assess the impact and success of these projects, we relied as much as possible on "hard" data: financial reports to show changes in cost effectiveness, survey data to show shifts in administrative and faculty attitudes, documents to record changes in institutional policy. But the process of evaluation—particularly the judgment of "success" or "failure"—is inevitably subjective, and we had to deal with more impressionistic data as well: the opinions expressed by a dean during an interview, our sense of faculty hostility toward a project director, our feeling that an administrator was "selling us a bill of goods" about the success of a project. Weaving together the hard and the soft data—the objective questionnaires and the subjective interview material, financial reports and firsthand observations, statistical evidence and visits, phone calls, and correspondence—we judge that, by and large, MIS and MBO can make a significant contribution to the management of liberal arts colleges and universities.

Unfortunately, fifteen of the forty-nine institutions lacked sufficient data for us to study: some of them had received their grants too recently to supply data: at others the projects were simply defunct, and no one was available to furnish data about them. Thus, in this book we must restrict most of our comments to the thirty-four institutions that were able to give us the information we needed by the end of our study period.

Even among these thirty-four institutions for which we have data, eight of them had received their grants so late in our study period that we could not evaluate their success; in Table 2, later in this chapter, we label these eight institutions as "too early to tell" about their success.

Nine of the thirty-four institutions, or 26 percent, had projects that, in our opinion, were outright failures. Some of these nine "least successful" projects did not even survive the end of their grant period. Others remained in existence in name only, with a director whose chief responsibility was some other task. Needless to say, these nine institutions showed little progress in improving their management behavior. Nonetheless, from interviews at these institutions, we derived valuable lessons about how *not* to implement management innovations—for example, that without administrative support and proper staffing, management innovations will fail; and much of the information in Chapter Eight on successful implementation of projects stems from these failures.

The remaining seventeen projects, or exactly half of all thirty-four for which we have data, were clearly and significantly successful. We base this judgment on a number of factors. First of all, these seventeen institutions had active management innovations under way. People in the institutions knew about the projects and were using them in decision making. They were actually gathering and using data more effectively ·than they had before. They were holding planning seminars and workshops. Their budgeting decisions were more often based on these data and on their planning activities. And not only the institutions' planning processes but their financial condition was improved. Not all these changes, of course, can be attributed only to the RAMP projects, but the projects undoubtedly had some impact on the changes.

Was a 50 percent success rate by the time our research ended a reasonable expectation for the Exxon Foundation? The answer here is, of course, a matter of judgment and perspective, but in our opinion a success rate of 50 percent in a complex program such as this is a highly respectable outcome—particularly when we consider that the overwhelming majority of innovations in higher education, as in most organizations, fail completely (see Baldridge and Deal, 1974). The reasons are numerous—among them, resistance by entrenched groups, inadequate technology, insufficient funding, and improper staffing. Hence, while it cannot be judged an unqualified achievement, we believe that Exxon's program was enormously beneficial to many of the participating institutions; and its success ratio was probably higher than that of most attempts to change management processes in higher education.

The data in Table 2, based on the responses of administrators to one of our questionnaires, illustrate several facets of the program's success. As the categories of projects show, those that we deemed successful included all types of RAMP innovation. Four of them involved only simple "data-bank" management information systems; seven involved "advanced" management information systems; and six focused on management by

Table 2. Percent of Administrators Agreeing with Questions by Different Categories of Project

	Category of Project				
	Least Successful (respondents at 9 institutions)	Too Early to Tell (respondents at 8 institutions)	Successful Data-Bank MIS (respondents at 4 institutions)	Successful Advanced MIS (respondents at 7 institutions)	Successful MBO (with MIS) (respondents at 6 institutions)
1. Project was very successful.	9	22	26	36	44
2. Project was moderately successful.	46	55	32	41	46
3. Project was disappointing.	18	0	16	0	0
4. Costs of the project were reasonable for the benefits received.	23	29	31	43	51
5. Project has become an integral part of the college management process.	18	27	31	57	72

objectives (MBO) in combination with MIS. The first three responses reported in Table 2 indicate the administrators' own ratings of their project's success. As can be seen, the institutions with MBO projects had the highest percentage of administrators reporting that the project was either very successful (44 percent) or moderately successful (46 percent). This total of 90 percent compares to a total of only 58 percent for basic "data-bank" MIS projects and 77 percent for "advanced" MIS projects.

An interesting phenomenon emerged from these answers: almost no one was willing to admit disappointment about a project. Even among those projects that we concluded were quite unsuccessful, only 18 percent of the administrators at these institutions agreed that their project was disappointing. None of the administrators at institutions with either advanced MIS projects or MBO projects were disappointed, but 16 percent of those with basic "data-bank" projects were disappointed, despite our own judgment that their projects were successful.

The answers to question 4 were also quite striking: the more successful a project (according to our own judgment), the more often the administrators think its costs are reasonable. Thus, at the colleges with unsuccessful projects, only 23 percent of the administrators felt that the cost was justified. By contrast, over half of those in institutions with successful MBO projects considered the cost reasonable. In response to question 5, 72 percent of the MBO administrators said that the project had become an integral part of the college management process. By contrast, only 18 percent of the administrators in the institutions with the least successful projects agreed.

Before we leave the general issue of project success, one other matter deserves attention. The fact that we rated a project "successful" might not mean that it was a leading light that should be followed and imitated by others. No, these judgments were always *relative to the unique situation*. We rated several projects "successful" that actually had very primitive management techniques and were quite unsophisticated. Their "success" lay in the fact that even these modest systems represented significant advances, compared to the even more primitive systems previously being used. Our "successful" case studies, then, vary enormously in the sophistication of their projects, but were all judged successful for their context, not necessarily as models for all higher education. The same caution is in order about the projects we rated "least successful." Even in these instances, we suspect that some institutions learned something—even if that was how *not* to run a management project. Let us not be Pollyannas and argue that even the failures were "really" successes— clearly, most were not. But the administrators with the least successful projects may have learned valuable lessons along the way, and perhaps their experiences prepared them for better future experiments.

Beyond these general conclusions about the impact and success of the RAMP projects, here are several specific findings that will be discussed in detail in later chapters.

1. *In successful projects the quality and quantity of data improved significantly.* In many cases this improvement was a matter of having data available on students, faculty, and budgets—data that simply did not exist before. In addition, the accuracy and availability of these data almost universally improved.

2. *The management innovations improved problem-solving capacities.* These improvements took several forms: (a) the speed of problem solving increased with the availability of good data; (b) the focusing of data on specific problems (a procedure we call "hot-spot analysis") was facilitated; and (c) the general level of management sophistication of the campus community increased.

3. *Institutions with successful MIS projects reduced variations in per student expenditures among departments.* In institutions with a vigorous management information system, departmental differences in expenditures were publicized, and variations in costs (dollars per student) among departments were reduced—primarily because expenses in the more costly departments were reduced and the student/faculty ratios equalized. In contrast, institutions that failed to implement an MIS project showed a continued pattern of wide variation among departments. However, there is no way of knowing exactly how much of this reduction in variation among departments is directly attributable to the MIS network (Chapter Six).

4. *Institutions with successful advanced MIS projects decreased their per student expenditures.* Our data suggest that

these successful projects helped cut per student expenditures, but we cannot tell conclusively whether the reduced costs resulted from the MIS or from other factors. For example, an institution aggressively trying to cut costs might also aggressively try to implement an MIS to help with the task, in which case aggressive management might account for both phenomena: the reduction in cost and the implementation of the MIS network. (This complicated issue of financial impact is discussed in Chapter Six.)

5. *MBO programs have unique strengths in improving the planning process.* A major conclusion from our study is that a data-based MIS can be significantly improved as a planning tool if it is linked to a vigorous MBO program. We were highly impressed with the successful MBO projects. They are particularly powerful in improving the planning process. In addition, when MBO projects are linked to an MIS program—as they all were under RAMP—they also capture the positive effects that an MIS program offers.

6. *Nonetheless, successful management innovations can have unanticipated and ambiguous consequences.* First, *adoption of an MIS will cause departments to maximize enrollments*, since faculty positions and other resources are directly tied to the number of student credit hours the department generates. Thus, departments may add new courses, eliminate courses that attract few students, and require students to take certain courses in order to increase enrollments. Second, *departments will try to minimize their indirect costs*—for example, by cutting back on counseling and other support services. Third, *departmental distrust may increase*, because departments are sometimes charged for services over which they have little control. Finally, *many management innovations will tend to centralize authority*, since information and planning may be centered in a few hands. Thus, it was disconcerting to find that faculty members, in particular, felt that power and authority on the project campuses were increasingly concentrated in the hands of the project administrators.

7. *The introduction of management innovations is a highly political process.* A management project may seem strictly routine and may even have an aura of "management science." But

we found that, in reality, most projects are highly charged politically and emotionally. People have their territories staked out,
and the introduction of new procedures and systems nearly always poses a threat to someone. In the successful projects in
our study, the project managers made a concerted effort to deal
with the political realities. Coalitions had to be built to support
the project: people with vested interests in the old system had
to be won over to the new procedures: committees had to be
persuaded that the innovation would benefit the college. Support had to be mustered throughout the college community.
Every successful project in our study had some political component. By contrast, the unsuccessful projects faced political opposition that was never effectively diffused. (Chapter Eight discusses the political characteristics of managerial innovations and
outlines some effective political strategies used in successful
projects.)

8. *Successful implementation involves a number of common features, and unsuccessful projects have common weaknesses.* The "success ingredients" include modest goals that do not
overpromise the results, a competent and well-trained full-time
staff, support of the top-level administration, effective funding
that does not starve the project, and widespread attempts to gain
faculty support. The "disaster ingredients" seem to be too much
turnover in project staffing, an absence of administrative support,
weak financial support, a scope of operation that is entirely too
broad and grandiose, an absence of faculty support, and a weak
base of management data. (Chapter Eight analyzes at length
both the "success" and the "disaster" ingredients.)

9. *One of the biggest problems of these management innovations is a failure to link planning activities with budgeting
strategies.* At project institutions, personnel often complained
that the MIS and MBO programs were undercut because they
were separated from established budgeting procedures. The information supplied by an MIS often came too late or was not
used appropriately for budget decisions, and the planning processes of an MBO sometimes had little impact on the budgetary
decisions (see Chapter Eight).

10. *A major problem beyond these management innovations is that instructional expenditures have been declining in al-*

most all institutions. One of the surprising conclusions of our budget analyses at project institutions is that, *when inflation rates are considered,* the money spent on direct instruction has · been steadily decreasing (Chapter Nine). Student/faculty ratios have increased, the number of faculty has declined, senior faculty have been replaced by junior faculty, and faculty salary increases have diminished. This decrease in instructional expenditures is apparent regardless of the type of management process the institution implemented. This is an extremely discouraging finding, especially in light of the public complaints about the high cost of education and the fact that academic programs will have to become more attractive as the number of students in the traditional age cohort declines.

11. *But the institutions with successful management innovations are using many strategies to increase their income and to cut expenses.* For example, many institutions have turned to the federal and state governments for additional income, although funds from both these sources will be harder to obtain as enrollments drop. New programs have been developed to attract nontraditional students, and new markets for students have been identified through planning and analysis. More effective admissions activities have been instituted—recruitment efforts monitored, enrollment goals projected, and performance measures generated. More effective development programs have been established to raise funds and generate support from various community groups. As with admissions activities, these programs have been monitored with performance measures. MIS projects have supported these programs with data such as alumni and student aid records. Many cost-reduction efforts have been directed at nonacademic functions: cutting fuel costs, trimming dormitory expenses, reducing secretarial and staff support, and lowering plant maintenance; student financial aid has also been cut back, since the gap between financial aid income and expenditures is a serious problem (Chapter Nine).

Before we turn to these detailed findings, one major question deserves answer here: Should institutions implement management innovations such as MIS and MBO with their own money? Our research staff has often been confronted with this query: "Getting a grant to implement MIS or MBO is great; but what if we have to do it with our own money—without a grant? Are the benefits worth the cost?" Our overall assessment, based on the facts in this book, is that the benefits of MIS and MBO are worth their cost if institutions are careful to structure these activities in a "lean" fashion—that is, (1) if existing staff are used and carefully trained; (2) if expensive new specialists are not hired to run the system but, instead, on-board people are retrained; and (3) if consultants are used carefully and economically and leave behind them a system that can be run by local people. We believe that these objectives can be met, and in Chapter Eight we enlarge on the subject of how to implement the projects.

Overall, it is our impression that management information systems and management by objectives programs are worth their cost. Throughout the book we will be explaining why we have reached this conclusion and what improvements result from them. Some institutions, however, let the bureaucracy and the mechanics of the system bog them down. They have hired expensive new staff when their own people could have done the job with a little training. They have paid consultants too much and got too little benefit. Thus, while the value of MIS and MBO is significant, there are pitfalls to avoid. The values and the pitfalls are the subject of this book.

Chapter Two

Improving
Management
Information

Management information systems (MIS) for colleges and universities have been around for over a decade. Although many people support MIS approaches, a large number of people also oppose them. In fact, there has been considerable controversy over the usefulness of MIS procedures in higher education. In a thoughtful article published in 1976, Paul J. Plourde commented on the debate:

> Considerable disagreement is raging about the applicability of these techniques to higher education administration. The primary issues are not new, and they have long been at the center of the ancient de-

Note: Some of the findings in this chapter have been reported in an article by other key researchers on the HERI project: Alexander W. Astin and C. E. Christian, "What Do Administrators Know About Their Institutions?" *Journal of Higher Education*, July/August 1977, *48* (4), 389–400.

14

bate between administrators in higher education.
Among these issues are the following.

- Defining and measuring education outputs
  are difficult tasks.
- The production functions of higher education are not concisely defined, and there
  is no accepted formula for determining
  the resources required to produce a unit
  of output.
- Quantifying basically subjective concepts
  such as the value added by the institution
  is a problematical task.
- Which is best: centralization or decentralization?
- There is an inherent conflict between administrative efficiency on the one hand
  and academic effectiveness on the other
  [Plourde, 1976, p. 18].

Not everyone agrees, however, that management information systems will not work. An increasing number of devoted administrators and institutional researchers believe that computerized data processing is the wave of the future for educational
decision making. These advocates believe that the opposition to
MIS programs is old-fashioned and muddleheaded. The 1971 report of the President's Task Force on Higher Education states
this position strongly:

> We are concerned about the widespread resis-
> tance to cost effectiveness thinking in higher educa-
> tion because it is so profoundly anti-intellectual. It
> rejects reason, and it puts a low value on the time
> of faculty trained to reason well. Faculties are an
> expensive resource, and concern over different ways
> of using their time does them honor.
>
> We must guard against the widespread ten-
> dency to trivialize the problem of efficiency in
> higher education. It is not only a financial problem
> but an intellectual one. The questions about effi-
> ciency lead to a host of questions about teaching
> and learning, and to the ultimate questions about

the nature and purpose of higher education. These
are too important to the colleges and universities—
and too intellectually challenging—to be lightly dis-
missed as illegitimate [Newman and others, 1971,
p. 32].

The debate rages on. Some people believe that management information systems will be the financial salvation of some
colleges and universities, that good data will help them back to
financial stability, and that decision making in academic circles
will become more rational. Other people believe that academic
values will be destroyed by too much emphasis on numbers and
that the subtle complexities of decision making will be ignored
by superficial analysis. In spite of this debate, almost all the colleges that received Exxon RAMP grants decided to implement
a management information system, even if they also used other
types of management innovations. In detailing its grant programs,
the Exxon Foundation had emphasized the need for decision
making based on first-class empirical data. Consequently, most
colleges established a data-gathering system and a procedure for
supplying the information to decision makers.

In this chapter, which explains how the institutions implemented these systems, we have three principal objectives. First,
we will set the stage with an elementary question: "Did the decision makers need the MIS projects, or was the information
already widely known?" This seems like a simple issue, but we
were not quite convinced that the data systems would make
much difference. We thought that many administrators would
already have the bulk of the information. So we decided to find
out just how much administrators knew about their institutions.
The first part of this chapter discusses the surprising level of *mis-*
information among administrators. It seems that they definitely
needed the help of the management information systems. Second, we will describe the basic types of management information
systems, which vary widely, each with a somewhat different purpose and procedure. A description of the major types and a comparison of their purposes should be helpful. Third, we will report
on what we learned about using these information systems. In
the course of our research, we saw many successful projects and

a fair share of disasters. Reflecting on what we saw, we will outline the lessons that can be learned for a more effective management information system.

Do Administrators Need Management Information Systems?

Most program planning and budgeting systems, management information systems, and other "modern" approaches to college management assume that an adequate knowledge of basic institutional data is essential for effective planning and decision making. A potential weakness in modern management is the large gap between the information gathered and stored on a computer tape and that which may actually get into an administrator's head. As the Exxon project began, we wondered whether new data systems, as proposed by many grant applications, were really needed. Was it not likely that many administrators *already* knew, through experience and long exposure to the institutions, the information that thousands of dollars would be spent to gather? We wanted to answer these simple questions: How much more do administrators know than other members of the institution? Are administrators more likely to know facts closely associated with their particular area of decision making?

Data were collected from administrators at twenty-three institutions that had received RAMP grants by the end of the 1974–75 academic year. Information about the administrators' knowledge of their institutions was obtained with self-administered questionnaires that were sent by mail and later collected by interviewers who visited each campus. Data were collected from the following administrators: president, academic vice-president, business officer, dean of students, director of development, admissions officer, financial aid director, and registrar. Each questionnaire had these directions: "We would like to find out which facts about your institution you have in your head. WITHOUT CONSULTING ANY OUTSIDE SOURCES, please give your best estimate for each of the following items. Then if you are not sure your estimate is correct, please provide the actual figures (if available) and the source."

Some of the questions were tailor-made to certain administrative positions. Questions about last year's operating surplus or deficit, for example, were asked of the chief fiscal officer but not of the registrar. In those tailor-made sections, we included only items that the particular administrator would be expected to know. In addition, several items common to all administrators were selected because they concerned the overall functioning of the institution and, presumably, related closely to such fundamental concerns as institutional survival. We assumed that any key administrators, regardless of their special functions, should be reasonably well informed on these items.

1. *Total enrollment.* For most private colleges today, maintaining adequate enrollments is the key to institutional vitality and survival. Thus, it seems reasonable to expect that virtually all administrators should know their institution's total enrollment.
2. *First-time enrollment.* This figure, the number of new students (freshmen) who had never before attended college, probably provides the best estimate of how successful the institution is in attracting new students.
3. *Continuing enrollment from previous year.* This information is critical in assessing institutional attractiveness to prospective students and in planning for student recruitment.
4. *Academic ability of entering freshmen—Scholastic Aptitude Tests (SAT).* These scores indicate the level of academic preparation of the entering class and are also regarded by some people as a measure of the institution's academic quality. On a more practical level, test scores help provide a basis for tailoring curricula to the academic need of the entering students.
5. *Percentage obtaining bachelor's degree in four years.*
6. *Faculty size.* This number is important not only because faculty represent the institution's major educational resource but also because faculty salaries are usually the largest single budgetary item.

Table 3 shows how accurately the different administrators recalled the basic items. The average percentage of error is given for each group. Thus, if a college's actual enrollment was 2,000 and the respondent's estimate was off by 100 (either 1,900 or

Table 3. Accuracy of Administrators in Recalling Basic Information
(N = 23 Institutions)

Administrator	(N)[a]	Mean Percentage Error in Recall							
		Enrollment (FTE)	Current First-Time Enrollment	Continuing Enrollment	Mean SAT or ACT of Freshmen Verbal	Math	Percentage Receiving Bachelor's in Four Years	FTE Faculty	All Items
Presidents	(16)	3	7	7	5	3	15	10	7
Chief academic officers	(17)	3	5	6	5	4	14	7	6
Chief fiscal officers	(18)	4	7	6	6	5	21	7	8
Chief student affairs officers	(20)	3	6	6	4	4	15	6	6
Directors of development	(14)	5	7	7	7	6	14	10	8
Directors of admissions	(21)	7	4	9	6	2	18	10	8
Directors of financial aid	(21)	6	6	8	7	6	17	19	10
Registrars	(19)	2	5	6	3	4	22	10	7
All administrators	(146)	4	6	7	5	4	17	10	7

[a]It was not possible to survey every administrator in all 23 institutions.

2,100), the error would be 5 percent. We then averaged the errors for all people in a group.

For several reasons the figures in Table 3 represent a *conservative* estimate of the error. First, the questionnaires were self-administered. There is no way to be sure that some administrators did not first consult outside sources for the answers, although they were specifically instructed not to do so. In at least one institution, the president's office circulated answers to some items before the interview team arrived on campus. Second, since it was sometimes difficult to discover the correct value, we averaged all the answers and took the average as our best guess of the "right" answer. This practice would, of course, minimize the overall error, because blatantly wrong answers would be figured as part of the "right" or average answer. Finally, since overestimates and underestimates were almost equally likely, two people committing a 5 percent error could differ by 10 percent (5 percent below the true figure, and 5 percent above = 10 percent difference). In short, the actual rate of error is probably much higher than Table 3 suggests.

Table 3 shows that administrators are *best* informed about the total enrollment of the institution (4 percent average error) and the academic ability of the entering freshmen (5 and 4 percent average error). Administrators are *least* informed about the percentage of students who received bachelor's degrees in four years (17 percent average error) and the number of faculty (10 percent average error). The best-informed administrators are chief academic and student affairs officers (6 percent error each); the administrators with the highest errors are the directors of financial aid (10 percent error). The differences are probably consistent with the realities of the different positions. With the exception of the president, the chief academic officer and the chief student affairs officer usually deal with a wider range of institutional programs than the other administrators.

Turning to the tailor-made questions for each area, differences in error among the various administrators are generally consistent with their traditional areas of responsibility. Thus, the registrars show the least error in reporting total enrollment, while the directors of admissions show the least error in reporting first-time enrollment. Student affairs officers and registrars show the best knowledge about SAT scores of the entering freshmen. The fact that registrars show the highest percentage of error with students who complete a degree in four years may be somewhat misleading. At only one of the 23 institutions was there agreement among administrators on the "correct" figure. Indeed, at some institutions there was more disagreement over the "correct" figure than in the original estimates. Clearly, the percentage of students completing a degree in four years is simply not known in most institutions, despite the obvious importance of this figure for institutional planning. Under these circumstances, it is possible that the registrars' estimates are actually closer to the true figure, in spite of their higher percentage of "error" when compared with the average scores. Such an interpretation is supported by the fact that registrars' estimates tend to be higher than those of other administrators in colleges with high completion rates, and lower in colleges with low completion rates.

The modest error in Table 3 might tempt one to conclude that most administrators are reasonably well informed about these basic facts and that perhaps they do not need the sophisticated data banks and computerized networks that management information systems provide. However, remember that we believe these error rates are *very* conservative and that the actual amount of misinformation is much higher. Moreover, a closer inspection of the data for individual institutions revealed several instances where the extent of misinformation is severe enough to make intelligent planning and dialogue about institutional problems very difficult, if not impossible. Case analyses for four such institutions (nearly one fifth of the sample) are presented below. The actual figures have been altered slightly to protect institutional anonymity, although the relationships (in terms of error in reporting) have been preserved.

Case 1. This is a relatively large institution of average selectivity located in a medium-sized city. Although the current freshman enrollment is 950 students, the president reports 1,350 students for *both* his original estimate and the "correct" value. Several other key administrators give similar high figures; the dean of one professional school, for example, reports 2,100 freshmen. With a freshman SAT verbal mean of 480, estimates range from 410 (academic officer) to 520 (director of development). The percentage of students completing degrees in four years is estimated from 40 percent (student affairs officer) to 80 percent (academic officer). The actual number of full-time-equivalent (FTE) faculty is 315; it is estimated between 285 (dean of a professional school) and 460 (president). The president reports 475 as the "correct" value.

   Case 2. This is a small, religiously affiliated institution in the suburbs of a large city. No one seems to know the total enrollment. Only the registrar gives the same figure, 975, for estimated and actual values. Initial estimates range from 940 (president) to 1,260 (four other administrators). All four administrators who give "actual" values report different figures, ranging from 975 (registrar) to 1,250 (director of financial aid). The current freshman enrollment is also unclear, although the correct figure appears to be approximately 270. Again, estimates vary by an astonishing rate, from 240 (director of development) to 440 (director of financial aid). The president's estimate is disturbingly high (380). Estimates of the previous year's freshman enrollment disagree by similar amounts. There is no consensus on the percentage of students receiving BA degrees in four years, and estimates range from 15 percent (director of planning) to 70 percent (registrar). Finally, despite the institution's small size, there is no agreement on the actual number of FTE faculty. Reports range from 30 (director of financial aid) to 70 (chief academic officer). The president's figure (55) occupies a middle ground.

   Case 3. This is a relatively large institution of moderate selectivity which offers graduate work in a number of professional fields. We suspect that the "correct" answers to most of the questions were circulated to all administrators before our site visit, because a large number of administrators give exactly the same figures for both estimated and actual values. Nevertheless, a number of startling disagreements occur. Most involve administrators who apparently did not receive the official figures. Thus, current freshman enrollment of 700 is estimated at 1,050 by the chief fiscal officer and 1,150 by the registrar. Both of these administrators give an identical figure (1,175) for the "correct" value, which is more than 50 percent greater than the "correct" value given by nine other administrators. The fiscal officer and the registrar also report a much larger previous year's freshman enrollment than the other administrators. Eleven administrators report the average SAT mathematics score as 530, but for those who evidently did not receive the "party line" figures, the estimates vary between 365 (dean of arts and sciences) and 570 (dean of a professional school). Although ten administrators report 55 percent as the "correct" figure for the proportion obtaining bachelor's degrees in four years, initial estimates range from 35 (student affairs officer) to 90 (director of financial aid). An FTE faculty of 410 is estimated as between 240 (director of admissions) and 405 (academic officer).

Case 4. This is a small, religiously affiliated institution in a rural area. While the administrators are in reasonably close agreement on total and first-time enrollments, there is extensive disagreement on the other items. The SAT mathematics mean for freshmen is estimated from 450 (registrar) to 550 (president), with reports for the "correct" value ranging between 345 and 500. Estimates of the percentage of students receiving bachelor's degrees in four years range from 40 (fiscal officer) to 85 (director of student life). Again, the president's estimate falls in between at 55 percent. No two administrators agree on the number of FTE faculty; estimates range from 70 (student affairs officer) to 120 (director of financial aid). Considering the relatively small faculty, the estimates of the president (90) and the chief fiscal officer (70) are disturbingly different.

While these examples represent the more extreme informational problems among our early Exxon institutions, several other institutions reveal potentially serious disagreements on particular items. One elite private college, for example, has large discrepancies among key administrators in the number of FTE faculty: estimates range from 280 (fiscal and academic officers) to 455 (president). The "correct" figures produce not a single case of agreement. Similarly, administrators at a predominantly black college vary in their estimates of the mean SAT mathematical score by some 200 points; their SAT verbal estimates vary by 125 points. Finally, administrators at one urban university disagree in their estimates of freshman enrollment by more than 2 to 1.

In addition to the common items asked all administrators, the responses of key fiscal managers (presidents, chief fiscal officers, directors of development and planning, and administrative vice-presidents) to the specific questions about the financial operation of their institutions reveal some potentially important weaknesses in the quality of information. Most administrators are able to quote quite accurate figures for their current institutional operating budget. However, one president and his chief fiscal officer disagree by $3 million on the size of a budget of approximately $20 million. At another highly prestigious institution, the vice-president estimates the budget at $45 million, the president at $48 million, and the chief fiscal officer at $53 million.

Even when the budget figure is well known, there can be a surprising lack of consensus on the *source* of income. One chief fiscal officer reports that the actual income from tuition and fees is 44 percent of the total budget. However, the president and the director of planning at the same institution report 63 percent and 41 percent, respectively, and both claim that the source of their actual figures is the business office. In an institution that says it is not merely in a "steady state" but in a "declining state," there are even greater discrepancies in the income attributed to tuition. The president estimates 85 percent, but the chief fiscal officer reports 59 percent; the information officer claims the actual amount from tuition is 73 percent. At another college seven top administrative officers estimate that tuition income ranges from 56 percent to 72 percent of the total; all seven figures are different.

Some errors in fiscal information may represent wishful thinking. For example, one president reports that gifts and contributions account for 10 percent of the total operating income, but his chief fiscal officer places the actual figure at 2 percent. Another president reports over $4 million in gift income, but the chief fiscal officer says that the true value is close to $1 million. At one institution with severe financial difficulties, the fiscal officer thinks that the budget deficit over the past two years has *increased* from $500,000 to $1 million, whereas the development officer reports that the deficit has *decreased* from $1 million to $600,000.

Even well-known, financially solvent institutions can be confused over a major point, such as the year-end budgetary surplus. In one case, the chief fiscal officer reports a surplus of $23,000, the president claims $10,000, and an academic vice-president estimates $8,000. Similarly, the amount spent for institutional research and development at one college is reported at $24,000 by the chief fiscal officer, $35,000 by the development officer, $40,000 by a vice-president, and $58,000 by the director of planning. Another development officer reports that his institution spends $300,000 for research and development when the most reliable information places the actual figure at only $42,000.

Clearly, there are major gaps in the information that administrators have about their institutions. Management information systems, of course, cannot completely solve that problem, but a good MIS network can substantially reduce the misinformation in an institution.

Closing the Information Gap with MIS

There has been a phenomenal growth in the number of institutions that use computer-based information systems to support various administrative functions. One survey of forty-eight large institutions indicated that administrative computing expenditures increased at an average annual rate of 33.4 percent between 1963 and 1968 and averaged 2.3 percent of an institution's total operating budget (Mann and others, 1975). A 1970 survey of 1,873 colleges and universities indicated that only 13 percent had some type of information system (Bogard, 1972). We estimate that about 50 percent of the institutions now have some type of computer-based information system, although they vary substantially in their sophistication. Such information systems are more likely to be used in large public institutions, although many small private colleges are trying to start programs.

Several types of computer-based information systems are currently in use. Some require extreme sophistication in the data base; others are simpler. Some systems incorporate many different types of data into one system—student data, financial information, personnel records. Other systems have each area in a different system; still others simply do not have much data. Some systems use the data primarily for current reports, with little impact on decision making. Other systems are highly integrated into the decision process, with advanced capacity to predict future impacts of current decisions.

Simple Data Banks

It would clear the air of much nonsense if everyone understood that the overwhelming majority of the so-called "management information systems" are really nothing more than simple data banks. Colleges have always gathered and compiled statistics about students, finances, faculty, alumni, and dozens of other items. In the early years, one of the cheerful, gray-headed ladies in the dean's office probably kept most records with a few sheets of paper in a notebook. When people needed to know something, they simply called her. As time passed and institutions became more complex, the data-gathering and statistical activities grew. Usually the left hand did not know what the right hand was doing. The admissions office kept one set of records, the financial office another, and the academic dean still another.

In recent years most institutions have established an office of institutional research. Now there is a full-fledged professional group called institutional research officers, with career patterns of their own, and an association—the Association of Institutional Research—where they can talk to each other. The research offices were established to consolidate the various statistics from all over the campus. The office serves as a focal point where information can be funneled, systematized, and translated into reports.

It is important to stress that, for the vast majority of colleges and universities, a discussion of a "Management Information System" would almost exclusively mean a discussion of the simple data banks compiled by the institutional research office. Using computers to compile these statistics has given the operation an aura of science and precision that the cheerful grayhaired lady and her dog-eared notebook never accomplished. However, the logic behind a fancy IR office and those pencil records is fundamentally the same. We call these simple management information systems *data-bank* networks.

These systems collect and store data, and they retrieve information for periodic reports. They may have many different data files on students, courses, personnel, financial accounts, and classroom space. The focus is on *collecting* data and producing simple reports, with little stress on *using* the data in the management process or on *predicting*. Consequently, these simple systems have limited applications for *analyzing* the data collected.

The technical characteristics of these systems have received considerable attention, especially the development of the software necessary to construct and maintain the data base (see Schroeder, 1972). The early versions of these data-management systems were essentially "self-contained" software packages that were applicable only to the *specific* data base (such as personnel records) for which they were developed. An early example was Stanford University's Information Network for Operations or INFO (Gwynn, 1969). Today a number of commercially developed data-management systems cover a broad spectrum. These systems are able to integrate data from, say, student records and faculty records, financial aid information, and admissions records. The ability to integrate different areas is a significant advantage. Examples of these more integrated data-management systems are IBM's Information Management System (IMS), Informatic's Mark IV, and CINCOM Systems' TOTAL. All these are all *general*-application data-management systems not limited to one area.

A number of problems must be solved before these simple data systems can be used.

1. *Data definitions must be standardized.* A constant plague of information systems is the lack of standardized terms. For example, what is a "student"? Are we talking about "body counts," full-time-equivalent students, students who have simply enrolled, or students who have persisted to some census date (such as ten weeks into the semester)? Unfortunately, different institutional offices often use different definitions, and the resulting figures may not be comparable. The same story holds true in dozens of operational areas. Before any meaningful statistics can be assembled, it is important that everyone compare apples to apples and oranges to oranges. The standardizing of

definitions is a difficult task, but it is a fundamental first step toward building any data system.

2. *The data must be clearly trackable.* Where do these data come from? That is a question every administrator has asked at one time or another—and has often been shocked to find that nobody knows the answer. To our surprise, "invisible sources" emerged as a serious problem on many campuses. Like a bastard child, reports sometimes arrive on a top administrator's desk without a clue to their original fathers. And when they *are* traceable, people are sometimes astonished at the amount of error, missing data, and simple sloppiness that colored the information. The neat, crisp numbers on the final report often cannot be traced to the real faculty members, the real students, the real classrooms, or the real dollars. Every system must have a clear flow chart that allows anyone to trace the final numbers back to the original sources.

3. *The information must be condensed.* In the early stages of building a system, the emphasis is almost always on *collecting* information. Later, however, it becomes apparent that the tons of information collected must undergo a process of condensation. How to condense, synthesize, and organize the information often becomes a highly debated issue. What one person needs condensed another person needs in raw form. But without condensation the data become utterly overwhelming. Having too much information is often as bad as not enough. We will discuss this issue later.

4. *The assumptions behind the data must be clearly stated.* Hundreds of decisions must be made in gathering data and preparing reports. Do part-time faculty count in the total number of faculty? Do they count on some fractional basis? Are laboratories counted the same as lecture halls? Does the School of Engineering define the student/faculty ratio in the same way as the School of Arts and Sciences? The list of possible decisions necessary for gathering data is endless. Unfortunately, many assumptions and decision points are lost. But the decision maker who receives the report *must* know the chain of assumptions that led to the numbers in that report.

These technical problems are common to all management information systems. They may seem like obvious matters, but anyone who has ever tried to implement a system knows that they are knotty, complex, and nasty problems. At times they seem to have a lifelike perversity in their ability to plague the system. Every time the definitions are standardized, someone will report the data in a different format. Every time the sources of information are pinpointed, a big gap will appear between the numbers and the real world. Every time the assumptions are finally uniform, somebody down the line will be on a different wavelength. These technical problems always arise even after people think they are long settled. It is no wonder people talk of the "ghosts" in their systems.

Advanced Management Information Systems

Advanced systems always incorporate simple data banks, but they add a major component: software to *simulate* the behavior of the institution by data manipulation. This simulation capability allows decision makers to ask "what-if" questions. For instance, it is possible to predict in advance, with fair accuracy, the cost implications of increases in the student/faculty ratio or to compare the cost implications of two different methods of changing the ratio. Plourde (1976) has reported that nearly 400 colleges or universities use some type of simulation model in planning. However, we are skeptical of those numbers, because respondents at only 186 institutions gave Plourde information— and about half of these gave incomplete information, and only a few said that the models were used frequently. In spite of the question about their use, however, these models deserve careful analysis, since many people have high expectations for their *future* usefulness.

John Keller, an early proponent of simulation models for decision making in higher education, has argued that these models will be useful in four different ways (summarized in Plourde, 1976, p. 20):

1. Development of the model automatically forces a deeper understanding of the interactions within the system under study; unsuspected attributes and linkages are discovered, and new insights into the real nature of the problem are fostered.

2. Models permit the evaluation of a wide range of alternatives—surely a key feature of cost-benefit analysis. . . .

3. Models help provide a hedge against risk and uncertainty. They are meant to answer the decision maker's perpetual question, "What if . . . ?" A model gives the decision maker a better idea of the degree of risk being undertaken, the possible penalties for being wrong, or the choices of alternatives with greater insurance features. . . . Where the variables are numerous or complex, a model can reveal the implications of changed inputs or assumptions in a way quite beyond the powers of the average decision maker.

4. Models are supposed to help cope with uncertainty.

Resource allocation models. The most common type of advanced information system is designed to improve the *allocation of resources.* The basic purpose is to predict the cost implications of changes in various institutional policies. Although there are important differences between specific models (which will be discussed later in this chapter), most resource allocation models share a common logic (see Hussain and Freytag, 1973).

First, these instructional cost models are all "student driven." The basic input is an estimate of the total number of students who will enroll in each academic department. These enrollment forecasts must consider such factors as the number of students who continue at the college, the number that transfer from other institutions, and the number of first-time students. Of course, these forecasts are affected by changes in the rate of unemployment, student dropout rates, and other factors. From where do these enrollment predictions come? In some cases the enrollment estimates are derived from student "flow models" that are part of the computer software. In other cases they are nothing more than the best guesses of various people on campus. Regardless of where they are derived, these enrollment estimates form the "demand" for resources in each department. The expected student enrollment is the base from which money is distributed.

The predictive models also relate the anticipated student enrollments to the *total work load* placed on the various departments. One method for establishing this relationship is to calculate an Induced Course Load Matrix (ICLM). The course matrix displays the average distribution of student enrollments, by major and class, in the lower- and upper-division courses of each academic department. Table 4 provides an example of an Induced Course Load Matrix. It shows the pattern of enrollment for the "typical" student in four "typical" departments. This table reveals that the typical lower-division history major enrolls in 11.8 semester hours of lower-division history courses, 4.2 semester hours of upper-division history courses, 3.9 semester hours of lower-division biology, and so on. The ICLM shows the typical flow pattern for any group of students—the departments in which they enroll and the number of courses they take.

The total work load for the various academic departments is the product of the estimated student enrollment (by major and level) and the average distribution of student course enrollment in the upper- and lower-division courses of each academic department. The resulting matrix, called the Instructional Work Load Matrix, is exemplified in Table 5. If the college estimated that there would be 143 lower-division history majors, and the average major enrolled in 11.8 semester credit hours (Table 4), a work load of 1,687 semester credit hours would be expected from these students. Repeating this process for other student majors and levels and summing across rows in Table 5 would provide the anticipated, lower-division departmental work load for the whole institution.

Once the total anticipated work load has been calculated for the various departments, the *costs* of operating each department can be estimated. These departmental costs are a function of institutional policies concerning the structure of the academic program (that is, the distribution of lecture and laboratory courses), average class size (for both lecture and laboratory sections), the number of courses that a faculty member is expected to teach, the amount of a faculty member's work load which is credited to laboratory as opposed to lecture courses, the rank distribution of faculty in each department, and the faculty

Table 4. Induced Course Load Matrix Showing Average Semester Credit Hours for "Typical" Student Majors in "Typical" Departments

Department	History			Biology			Fine Arts			Business		
	LD	UD	GD	LD	UD	GD	LD	UD	GD	LD	UD	GD
History												
Lower division (LD)	11.8			6.7			6.0	4.3		4.6	1.9	
Upper division (UD)	4.2	11.3	4.5		4.5		2.3	7.6	7.4	2.3	6.1	4.7
Graduate division (GD)			18.3		3.9	2.1						
Biology												
Lower division (LD)	3.9	4.1		12.5	13.7		4.2	4.1		5.4	4.0	2.8
Upper division (UD)				5.8	2.1			2.0	1.3			
Graduate division (GD)						20.4						
Fine Arts												
Lower division (LD)	3.7	2.7		2.7	1.8		10.9			.6	3.5	
Upper division (UD)		6.5	3.0		3.5	2.9	6.3	10.3			1.4	1.3
Graduate division (GD)									19.3			
Business												
Lower division (LD)	6.4	2.8		2.3	.5		.3	1.7		12.8	1.1	
Upper division (UD)		2.6	4.2						2.0	4.3	10.3	
Graduate division (GD)						4.6					1.7	21.2
Total annual semester-hour load	30.0	30.0	30.0	30.0	30.0	30.0	30.0	30.0	30.0	30.0	30.0	30.0

Note: FTE student load equals thirty annual semester hours.
Source: Clark and others (1973).

Table 5. Instructional Work Load Matrix Showing Anticipated Semester Credit Hours for Student Major in Selected Departments

Department	History			Biology			Fine Arts			Business			Total
	LD	UD	GD	LD	UD	GD	LD	UD	GD	LD	UD	GD	
History													
Lower division (LD)	1,687			811	423		510	262		828	391		4,912
Upper division (UD)	601	2,102	234		367	95	195	464	126	414	1,257	583	6,438
Graduate division (GD)			952										952
Biology													
Lower division (LD)	558	763		1,512			357	251	22	972			4,435
Upper division (UD)				702	1,288			122			824	347	3,283
Graduate division (GD)					197	918							1,115
Fine Arts													
Lower division (LD)	529	502		327	169		926			108	721		3,283
Upper division (UD)		1,208	156		329	130	536	628			288	161	3,436
Graduate division (GD)									328				328
Business													
Lower division (LD)	915	521		278	47		26	103		2,304	227		4,421
Upper division (UD)		484	218			207			34	774	2,122		3,839
Graduate division (GD)											350	2,629	2,979
Anticipated student enrollment	143	186	52	121	94	45	85	61	17	180	205	124	
Total annual semester-hour load	4,290	5,580	1,560	3,630	2,820	1,350	2,550	1,830	510	5,400	6,180	3,720	39,420

Source: Clark and others (1973).

salary schedule. In addition, these instructional cost models can allocate the costs associated with nonfaculty expenses such as nonacademic personnel, departmental supplies, and equipment. By manipulating these policy variables, the resource allocation model can assess the cost implications of managerial changes. For example, an advanced MIS network could predict the cost of changing faculty work load or average faculty compensation.

Finally, these resource allocation models produce a common set of output reports. These output reports may be combined to produce information on the direct costs of each academic department or program. Some resource allocation models can also allocate *indirect costs* (such as libraries or counseling services) to departments, but because this capability is not widely used, we will focus on direct costs only.

Comparison of Resource Allocation Models. It is important to note some fundamental differences among the more common resource allocation models in use. One of the earliest resource allocation models was the Comprehensive Analytical Methods of Planning in University Systems (CAMPUS), developed by the Systems Research Group of Toronto (Judy, 1969; Levine, 1969). The CAMPUS model has gone through a number of revisions, the latest being a package known as CAMPUS IX. The CAMPUS model deviates from the basic logic of other resource allocation models in two important ways (Hussain and Freytag, 1973). First, the estimation of departmental work load is calculated in "contact hours," a procedure that requires a substantial increase in the data requirements (Weathersby and Weinstein, 1970; Schroeder, 1972). Second, the CAMPUS model allows for more variables to be manipulated by the user (Weathersby and Weinstein, 1970; Hussain and Freytag, 1973). For instance, instead of just estimating the average class size, the CAMPUS model can consider such variables as the minimum and maximum class size and the maximum number of courses. Again, the increase in flexibility is acquired at the expense of additional data requirements.

The second major resource allocation model in use is the Resource Requirements Prediction Model (RRPM), developed by the University of California and now available from the National Center for Higher Education Management Systems

(NCHEMS). RRPM has also undergone a number of revisions, the latest being RRPM 1.6 (Clark and others, 1973). Although RRPM is similar in logic to the resource allocation models discussed above, several characteristics should be noted. First, compared with CAMPUS, the data requirements for operating RRPM are much less complex. The tradeoff for this reduced data requirement is less detailed information. Thus, RRPM is less flexible than CAMPUS, for the user is limited to the analysis of costs for academic *departments*, while CAMPUS gives information about each *course*. Compared with CAMPUS, then, RRPM requires less (and less costly) data but cannot give such detailed information.

Another resource allocation model, the System for Evaluating Alternative Resource Commitments in Higher Education (SEARCH), was developed by the accounting firm of Peat, Marwick, and Mitchell for use in small institutions. This model differs from those discussed above in a number of ways. First, it reports data only for large units (such as the School of Liberal Arts or the School of Business). Second, SEARCH conceptualizes the college as consisting of five components: students, programs, faculty, facilities, and finances. In the finance component, SEARCH deviates from most other resource allocation models (Weathersby and Weinstein, 1970) by allowing the user to conduct an extensive analysis of *revenues* (income) as well as *expenditures* (outgo). Although knowledge of the relationship between income and expense is extremely important for most institutions, this link is unavailable in most other MIS programs.

Among other resource allocation models, Michigan State University has developed an extensive computer simulation model (Koenig, 1969; Weathersby and Weinstein, 1970), and models also have been developed by the Kansas City Regional Council for Higher Education, Tulane University, and the University of Washington (Weathersby and Weinstein, 1970; Schroeder, 1972; Gray, 1976a). These models have generally been confined to the institution for which they were developed and thus do not have as wide an application as the CAMPUS, RRPM, and SEARCH models.

Other Types of Models. In addition to resource allocation models—programs that help make decisions about budgets and money—there are several other kinds of advanced management information systems: student flow models, faculty flow models, and space utilization models.

Student flow models are concerned with three fundamental processes: (1) the prediction of student enrollments, (2) student progress within the institution, and (3) the student enrollment status at the end of each academic term. In each case the task is to predict future trends, based on past experience and an assessment of changing conditions.

Faculty flow models are intended to assist administrators in determining the composition of faculty by rank, age, discipline, and salaries (see Weathersby and Weinstein, 1970; Schroeder, 1972; Gray, 1976b). Simulations help provide information to answer policy questions: the rate of faculty promotion, the proportion of tenured faculty, or the impact of institutional retirement practices. Faculty employment patterns are likely to change rapidly over the next few years, because student enrollment in higher education is expected to decline significantly. Because this type of information can help predict the impacts of retrenchment, retirement, and tenure trends, these simulation models are likely to draw increased attention in the next few years.

Space utilization models received considerable comment in the 1960s due to the expansion of higher education in that "golden era." Because this expansion was anticipated, the basic concepts and definitions for facility planning were well established before 1960 (Russell and Doi, 1957). Computer-based simulation models have assisted administrators in making these expensive and often irreversible decisions. Such models are exemplified in the work of Arcuri and associates (1969) and Romney (1972). Further, several of the resource allocation simulation models discussed above contain space utilization modules as part of the overall package.

Lessons to Be Learned

The Nature of the MIS Project

Obviously, the nature of the management information project will largely determine whether it does the job. In the

Exxon program many different types of projects were selected. Some were sophisticated computer-based management programs, while others stressed setting institutional planning and objectives. Although the projects were quite different, certain rules apply to almost all of them.

The project must fit the institution's needs. Consultants sometimes try to sell their bag of tricks (in this instance, prepackaged computer programs) without serious assessment of the institution's situation. This was particularly true for the institutions that adopted management information systems. Like a traveling dog and pony show, the consultants pushed prepackaged computer programs that were supposed to do the job. In many cases, however, the prepackaged programs did not meet the college's needs. The prepackaged management information systems were usually developed at large institutions with thousands of students and faculty and complex administrative arrangements. When small colleges bought the prepackaged programs with their Exxon grants, they quickly found that systems designed for large institutions were not easily adapted. The lesson is simple: An institution should buy a management information system appropriate to its specific needs. This rule also applies to the other types of management innovations, such as management by objectives (MBO). However, the most complaints were voiced about the software packages of management information systems, not about the planning and workshop activities of the MBO systems.

The data base should be built slowly and steadily: crash programs usually do not work. In almost all the projects funded by Exxon, there was some data-gathering component. Even where MBO programs were started, they were usually supplemented with data gathering. We found great variations among the institutions. Somewhat over half appeared to have adequate data bases; the rest found that their data were either nonexistent or in such poor condition that they had to be substantially revised. But crash programs to improve the data base are rarely effective. Instead, the most successful programs build their data gradually over a long period. Of course, this is discouraging news for an institution that does not already have a good data base. Nevertheless, institutions should be skeptical of mounting man-

agement information systems without first giving careful attention to the data base underlying the program. In many cases the
administrators felt that a computerized capacity for *processing*
the data was a problem. But it appeared to us that the underlying process of *gathering* quality data in the first place was often
the faulty link. In short, a strong infrastructure of high-quality
data must be built before any attempts to superimpose a sophisticated processing system.

The program should be kept simple. A little sign sat on
the desk of a president we interviewed: "KISS." "What does that
mean?" we asked. "Keep It Simple, Stupid!" was the answer.
The advice is well taken for everyone who launches these projects. Where projects failed, the universal complaint was that
they had "gotten out of control," that complexity had mush-
roomed. The project director at one of the larger institutions
commented on the matter: "If I had this project to do over
again, what is the most important single thing that I would
change? Reduce the complexity of it! We threw in everything
but the kitchen sink. We proposed that we would introduce new
software, develop new planning programs, and supply planning
data for the trustees. Our promises looked like mountains, our
performance like mole hills. We ran in every direction at once.
It seemed we would never focus on one problem long enough to
solve it. The complexity of the damn project got totally out of
control. Judged against that kaleidoscope of objectives, we were
a failure. Had we had fewer objectives and a simpler project, we
probably would have been judged a success."

In his survey of 186 campuses that used different simulation models, Plourde (1976, p. 30) reported that many respondents consider their programs too complex:

> The findings of this research effort do *not*
> substantiate the need for more sophisticated mod-
> els. The comments of many of the respondents in-
> dicate just the opposite need, namely, to simplify
> the available models and reduce the volume of com-
> puter output that the various systems produce. Here
> are some typical comments:
> - The key problem is not with the technical
>   aspects of models, but with fostering their

use. A better understanding of how these tools have been used by others would be of great help.

- Models must be much less detailed and complex than the one we used.
- The institution must choose the questions to be answered, not the designer or programmer.
- Models rapidly become too complex . . . and [they become] confused with the real world in the eyes of the user.
- There has been a tendency of vendors to oversell the models. They never fully describe the work it takes to establish the data for these models.
- Analytical models should be advertised as only aids in decision making. Do not oversell as the answer to all problems.

Routine Behavior of the Project Unit

Are there any lessons that we can learn about the routine behavior of the project? From our questionnaires and on-site studies, we believe that some patterns of operation are more successful than others. Let us examine some of these routine patterns.

"Information glut" is a terrible temptation. In every project—whether it was an MIS or an MBO program—there was a fatal tendency toward "information glut." A new project director invariably wants the project to have high visibility among the faculty and administrators. As a consequence, there is an extensive buildup of newsletters, memos, directions for activity, and planning documents: "Hey, look at us, we've got a new thing going." In the process of gaining visibility, the information overload grows.

With management information systems, there is a particular tendency toward information glut. In those programs a computer chained away in some dark dungeon is always spewing tons of printout. Then little dwarfs in black cloaks wheel the sacred printout around to various administrators and dump it on their desks. Time after time we saw frustrated administrators sitting

behind piles of computer paper, afraid to ignore the sacred tab-
lets, insecure about reading the foreign language, and frightened
to perform the logical—but sacrilegious—act of throwing it away.
They simply did not know how to deal with the information
overload. The wise director of a management information system
quickly learns that too much information is as bad as not enough.

In some cases information glut can be more than a nuis-
ance; it can be used as a weapon to hide important facts. A snow
job with fancy data is still a snow job. One dean of a northeast-
ern college told us, with a sly wink, the following story: "I've
learned an important tactic from all this management information system business. People used to criticize me for not giving
them enough information. Faculty members used to bombard
me with complaints that I was hiding facts from them. Now
I give them *all* the information—bundles and bundles and bundles. I'm hiding the real information better than I ever did before! There is so much junk that I throw at them, they can't tell
the important stuff from the trivial stuff. And, sure as hell, nobody can say I am not giving them enough information!" This
dean had learned one of the classic ploys of the military secret
service: The best way to hide a secret is to surround it with junk
data. Overload the circuits with static. Give the enemy so much
stuff, false and trivially true, that he or she will not know which
information to act on. Winston Churchill was once quoted on
this issue: "The truth is so important [that] it must be accom-
panied by a bodyguard of lies."

The moral of the story is clear: Unless the data are condensed and focused on specific issues, they are virtually useless.
Project directors sometimes complain that administrators are
not using their output. When examined closely, this complaint
often means that the project directors are simply inundating the
administrators with unfocused, unsynthesized, undigested, and
uncondensed junk.

The data must be timely. One frequent complaint about
the Exxon projects was rather surprising. People said that the
critical data from the management information system came
after the decisions were made. And in some management by objectives programs, the planning cycles and the workshops that
were supposed to produce plans did not match the budget cy-

cle's timing. The planning was sometimes done *after* the budget process had occurred. These seem like absolutely ridiculous cases of mistiming. We could not imagine any sensible administration running an elaborate planning process that did not match the budget timing. And the production of MIS reports after the decisions were made seemed equally wasteful.

There are many explanations for mistiming. Usually, it means that the left hand doesn't know what the right hand is doing. For example, the management information system might be so isolated organizationally that the program director does not know when people need the information. Or, in other situations, an MBO planning project may be run by a person who has little input into the budgeting process. To paint a more sinister portrait, some administrators *deliberately* cause mistiming so that the planning *cannot* affect budgets—which the administrator wants to control. Under those circumstances, it is no surprise that the planning and the budgeting processes do not go forward together.

The simple conclusion is that the production of data in a management information system, or the planning cycle in a management by objectives program, must carefully match the decision-making and budgeting cycles. This obvious point is overlooked because of lack of coordination, incompetence, or political expedience. Nevertheless, anyone running a project should pay careful attention to timing and coordination.

Finally, accurate, focused, and timely data are expensive. Hopkins (1974) indicates that the cost of implementing a cost simulation model is approximately $75,000, a large portion of which is consumed by the gathering of data that meet specific requirements. Further, an adequate data base is subject to Gresham's Law: routine data maintenance tends to foreclose opportunities to extend and refine the basic data base. Yet, these costs must be borne because an adequate data base is the sine qua non of a cost simulation model.

Project directors must work closely with administrators to frame the right questions. A critical element in the implementation of a computer-based model concerns the expertise to operate such models. Such expertise may be present on campus, or it may be a service provided from external consultants. Plourde

(1976) reports that the presence of in-house technical expertise
was considered to be among the top factors in successfully implementing a cost simulation model. However, in-house expertise is not without its problems. Listen to the academic dean of
a southern college:

> We worked hard to develop a first-class data
> base and an excellent software system. But in spite
> of that, in the early stages we had a hell of a problem
> getting the appropriate information. After a while
> we realized the difficulty: the project director was
> giving us answers to questions we weren't asking!
> And, more often than not, when we asked a ques-
> tion, he did not furnish appropriate data. He had
> his own idea of what we needed and was giving us
> tons of information about it. But we usually wanted
> something else. Wow, the amount of miscommuni-
> cation over this problem was unbelievable. Finally,
> the president called the committee together, and
> for about six weeks we thrashed through the kinds
> of information we needed and wanted. We insisted
> that the *amount* be reduced and the *focus* be on
> things we really needed. After that the situation
> got dramatically better.

Again, the project's staffing and the administrative location are critical. If the director is located close to the people using data from the project, there may not be a problem. However,
if projects and users are not closely linked, there is a strong
temptation to design grand plans or produce great quantities of
information that have virtually no relation to the real decision-
making world. The *linkage* between the project directors and
the users of the project data is critical.

It is important to realize that this is also a two-way street.
The dean quoted above was criticizing the project director for
not giving him the right information. He implied that he finally
got the project director straightened out. But in other cases we
saw instances where the administrators really did not know what
they wanted. They often made floundering attempts to understand the planning process or data gathering, but they were so

inept that they only made matters worse. A common mistake by administrators was to ask for specific information without explaining *why* the data were needed or what the *question* was. Often an institutional researcher could have helped much more with *other* relevant data, if he or she had only known the question and the full background. The project directors probably have a responsibility to help the administrators frame their questions. However, they often feel ambivalent about this problem, as one explained in an interview: "As project directors, we don't know whether we should play an 'active' or a 'passive' role. We are supposed to be serving the faculty, the administration, and the trustees. We certainly have an obligation to help them understand the planning process or the use of data in decision making. But how far should we go? If we get too pushy, we might actually be making a lot of the critical decisions. On the other hand, if we play the role too passively, we fail to help people frame the right questions or plan more comprehensively."

It is almost impossible to specify exactly how a communication linkage should be built. In some cases the project directors should be aggressive in helping administrators and faculty understand the planning process and the use of data. In other cases administrators will have to reach out, insisting that the project directors concentrate on real problems rather than spinning out endless reports with no focus. The exact style is open to question, but it is clear that two-way communication must be established.

Purchasing this expertise from an outside consultant is subject to these same communication problems. Organizational consultants tend to bring specific biases and procedures to bear on these problems (Baldridge and Deal, 1974). As a result, consultants tend to (1) claim that their models can do more than they can, (2) create an appearance of certainty, and (3) be too technique oriented (Kirshling, 1976). However, consultants can be invaluable in reprogramming their software to meet the needs of the institution and in training on-site personnel in the use of these models. This latter aspect is particularly important in ensuring the institutionalization of such models once the model is implemented and consultant services are terminated.

Once a system has been implemented, the information must be used in making a decision. Cost simulation models do not *make* resource allocation decisions. Such models are designed only to answer "what-if" questions posed by institutional decision makers (Mason, 1975). Further, such information is typically only one of many inputs into such decisions. Because these models do not make decisions, the implementation of such a model presupposes that campus administrators are motivated to use it (Katz and Kahn, 1975). To supply this motivation, it has been argued that administrators should be *involved* in the implementation of these models (Brady and others, 1975), thus becoming aware of both the strengths and weaknesses of the model and the assumptions on which projections are based. The myth that an administrator does not have to understand how a model works, only how to use it, should be exposed for the fictitious entity that it is.

Pitfalls in the Process

We would like to add a warning about three common pitfalls. First, always be skeptical and alert about the quality of data: they are often wrong in spite of their surface precision. Second, the use of statistics and data is a highly *political* enterprise, in spite of its seemingly "scientific" nature. Third, there is a seductive temptation to count as important only those things that are concrete and measurable and that can be neatly tabulated even if they are trivial. Let us look more closely at these problem areas.

The data from a management information system often appear completely scientific. The columns of numbers and pages of printout almost assume a reality of their own. Rather than mere facts *about* the real world, they begin to look as though they *are* the real world. There is a seductive quality to this numbers game. People begin to believe that the numbers are hard facts, that the pages of printout somehow come from God. We believe, however, that this deification of numbers is one of the most common mistakes in using an MIS. No matter how scientific these numbers look, there is an amazing amount of sloppiness behind every printout. Remember the long chain of events from collection to printout. The data must be collected by forms that are filled out by students, faculty, secretaries, clerks, administrators, and janitors. Many data are missing or incorrect. People often make errors when the different sources of information are merged. It is not at all unusual for batches of data simply to get lost in the process. The list of accidental goof-ups that threaten the quality of data could be extended indefinitely. This does not mean that MIS networks are more prone to mistakes than other inventions of mankind, but neither does it mean that these systems are *less* prone to sloppiness.

There is no need for overanxiety about data quality; we do not want to overdo this caution. Becoming paranoid would be just as false as being overconfident. Nevertheless, any intelligent user of an MIS must constantly raise questions about the quality of the data. Are they accurate? Are they comprehensive? Is all the material there? Have major pieces of information been lost? Is everyone who contributes to the data base using the same definitions? Can the data be tracked to their source if necessary? The quality of data simply cannot be assumed. There must be unending war to make sure they are clean, accurate, and comprehensive. Eternal vigilance is, we are told, the price of liberty; good data cost the same.

Beware of politics of numbers. In the preceding section we outlined some ways accidents happen, and data become faulty because of mistakes. In this section, we want to turn to *deliberate* misuses of data. The data that look so scientific are often utterly rife with political manipulations. In our interviews with Exxon representatives and campus administrators, we came across scores of cases where people had learned to play the "numbers game." The best way to explain this point is to take two examples.

First, let us examine the affirmative action program of a college in the Southwest. The community where this college is located has three major racial groups: white, Mexican-American, and black. In preparing the affirmative action plan to meet federal guidelines, the college used data from its management information system. The guidelines said that the college must try to employ the "same percentage of each racial group as exists in the community." The numbers game was played with the concept of "community." The locale immediately around the college was predominantly white; the city where the college was located had a large number of blacks; and the surrounding five-county area was heavily Mexican-American. The task of the MIS seemed simple: to supply the "equal percentage" that matched the college work force with the local community. A computer printout was produced which showed how many members of each racial group should be hired by each department. Then the controversy erupted. What was the "community" on which this printout was based? People who wanted to keep the college employees limited to whites insisted that the college "community" was the area within a mile or so around the campus. Black civic groups, however, insisted that the appropriate reference "community" was the city—but not the county. Mexican-American civic groups demanded that the "community" be the five-county area around the institution. And one top administrator, who wanted to keep things essentially the same, grandly declared that the college's "community" was the entire United States and that the college already met the principle of equality for that reference group. The director of the MIS program, who had rather naively produced a document based on the idea that the city was the appropriate reference group, ran into an immediate hailstorm of criticism from everybody except the black groups, who were pleased at the choice. The numbers looked concrete and scientific, but the source of those numbers became a political hot potato.

A second example of the "politics of numbers" was given to us by the institutional research director at a large public university. Although that institution did not have an Exxon RAMP grant, the illustration is pertinent here. This university had an opportunity to secure federal grant money if it had a substantial group of American Indians or "Native Americans." The institutional research director explained how he moved the institution from a point where it received almost no funds to a position where it obtained over a quarter-million dollars a year. When students enroll, they are asked to specify their race on an information sheet. For years the question had these options: white, black or Negro, Chicano, American Indian or Native American, other. To increase the number of American Indians appearing in the statistics, the research director retitled the choice "Native American" and moved it to the head of the list. The number of "Native Americans" who went to this university increased fifteenfold in one semester, and the university became eligible for substantial federal grants. To give the devil his due, it is only fair to mention that the university really did undertake a sustained recruiting effort for American Indians at this time. But nobody could believe that the campus had increased its group of Native Americans fifteen times over.

Examples of the numbers game could be multiplied a hundred times over. There is the college president who deliberately clouds the distinction between "FTE students" and "student head count" to make people believe that his college is bigger than it actually is. We know of another incident where an institutional research director "lost" over 500 "class drop cards" just as the attendance census was being taken by the state auditors. These cases of blatant misrepresentation are fairly rare, but the more subtle types of change, manipulation, and distortion go on all the time. Charts, for example, can be prepared so that small changes look enormous—a ploy that every muckraking journalist in the world well knows. The old saying stands: "Statistics never lie, but statisticians certainly do." This warning applies with a vengeance to the political manipulations surrounding a management information system.

Do not be tempted by the tyranny of the concrete. A nasty myth abroad in the land suggests that something is real only if it can be measured, kicked, spat on, and reduced to numbers on a chart; that such things as insight, feelings, judgment, and subjectivity are *not* real. That myth has wormed its way into the heads of a large number of otherwise sensible and sane college administrators. We know administrators who would become violently angry if we accused them of being superstitious. But we have watched those same administrators get down on their knees before the altar of data and go through the most bizarre ritual acts.

Unfortunately, the availability of computerized data systems helps promote the silly notion that things are important if they can be measured, counted, and reduced to computer printout. Let us be clear about our value judgments here. We feel very strongly that adequate data and a good management information system are invaluable aids to decision making. We do not wish to join the camp of know-nothings who attack data-based decision making—usually because they do not understand it. But we also insist that data systems and their outputs have sharp limits to what they can do. And that is the point we are emphasizing here.

We can illustrate this problem from our own research. At the Montreal meeting for the Association for Institutional Research in the spring of 1977, we gave a conference session on our research. We reported the various trends we saw developing and the various promises and problems involved in the system. We had just completed a round of hundreds of intensive interviews on the campuses. In addition, we had just completed a huge computer analysis of questionnaires from the various administrators. We tried to blend together the results from our interviews and questionnaire studies—the same thing we are doing in this book. After the conference session, the president of a college came up to talk about the issues. In discussing the matter, we told him about a particular problem that had emerged from our interviews. Finally, he turned away and said in a rather disgusted voice, "Don't give me all those opinions—I want the *hard facts* that came from your computer analysis."

In short, he was playing the "tyranny of the concrete" game. Somehow the *opinions* of administrators expressed in short-answer questionnaires and reduced to numbers were more real to him than the same *opinions* expressed in intensive interviews where we could probe in depth. To our minds we had learned at least as much about the process from the interviews as from the "hard data." But to this man's mind, the only reality was the one that could be expressed in numbers. The same subtle threat exists whenever an MIS is used.

Serious decision making requires a skillful blend of data-based judgments, subjective evaluations, historical perspectives, and an appreciation of political realities. There are *many* inputs into the decision process. Data from an MIS is only one. To treat the data with respect and appreciation is a move toward intelligent decision making, but to treat the data as sacred cows is the surest way to disastrous decisions.

Summary

We have tackled several tasks. First, we suggested that there is a remarkably high level of *mis*information abroad on most campuses. To a surprising degree, administrators are unclear about some central pieces of information. Second, we described some of the management information systems that can help close the information gap. Finally, we examined some lessons that can be learned about managing an MIS. The MIS itself must be appropriate to the institution's needs and must produce high-quality information. Moreover, the routine activities of the project must be carefully arranged. The data must be timely, condensed, focused on real problems, and addressed to questions that people need answered. The proper use of an MIS also requires that the quality of the data be jealously guarded, that their political uses be recognized and guarded against, and that the "tyranny of the concrete" not be allowed to warp decisions.

Chapter Three

Developing Management Information Systems

Introducing MIS: A Case Study

Founded by Methodist leaders in 1831, Wesleyan University, in Middletown, Connecticut, seemed destined to remain yet another small, New England liberal arts college. A combination of unusual circumstances, however, has made Wesleyan one of the leading liberal arts universities in the United States. Today, a combination of circumstances threatens the ability of Wesleyan to maintain this leading position.

The foundation for Wesleyan's national reputation was a spectacular growth in the value of Wesleyan's endowment. First, an aggressive investment policy in common stocks was instituted during World War II, in anticipation of a postwar inflationary period. Second, the university received two bequests in the early 1950s totaling more than $8.5 million. But most impressive was the acquisition by Wesleyan of the American Edu-

50

cation Publications or "The Press." By the time Wesleyan sold "The Press" to the Xerox Corporation in the 1960s, it had realized more than $100 million from this publishing venture. On a per student basis, the value of Wesleyan's endowment exceeded that of Harvard.

One manifestation of the spectacular growth in Wesleyan's financial aspects was the expansion of the physical plant. While most of its buildings date back to Wesleyan's youth, there have been at least ten major additions since the late 1950s. The total value of these additions exceeds $59 million. Today the architectural style varies widely, extending from the earlier ivy-covered brick structures to the modern science center and the center for the arts. The indebtedness from the construction of the arts center is viewed by some faculty members as evidence of financial mismanagement.

The possession of such a substantial financial base has also encouraged a great deal of innovation in Wesleyan's academic program. The basic educational philosophy of Wesleyan is that "students should mature in an atmosphere of freedom and responsibility." Thus, students are allowed to design their own courses of study. However, they must design their program in consultation with a faculty adviser to ensure that they get a liberal education, not just a random collection of courses. As the Wesleyan catalogue says, "Intensive work and a degree of discipline mastery in a major field of learning provides one indispensable dimension of a liberal education." Thus, the undergraduate curriculum has both depth and breadth. Courses are divided into five major areas: the arts, languages and literature, social studies, philosophy and religion, and sciences and mathematics. Students are encouraged to select about one third of their courses in one of these areas of inquiry and to explore the remaining areas. In addition to concentrating their programs in traditional academic departments, students may also concentrate in interdepartmental major programs, such as American studies and classical studies.

Wesleyan considers its "College Plan" its best-known innovation in the liberal arts curriculum. The College Plan includes the College of Letters and the College of Social Studies, where students are involved in a heavy reading and writing schedule under scrutiny by faculty tutors. Instead of regular classroom schedules, grades, and testing, students are expected to complete a major thesis in their senior year and to pass a comprehensive examination given by outside examiners.

A small number of "advanced learning" or graduate programs complement this undergraduate curriculum. Due to its great wealth, Wesleyan began recruiting a highly talented faculty throughout the 1950s. This recruitment policy resulted in faculty pressures to develop a "Little University," which would contain a small number of distinguished doctoral and advanced studies programs, such as the Center for the Humanities. While the faculty stressed that the 1962 transition to the concept of "Little University" would enrich the undergraduate experience, members know that such a conception of Wesleyan would also encourage the faculty's scholarly pursuits.

Over the last ten years the average age of a faculty member has remained essentially unchanged, as has the percentage of faculty with doctorates. However, the faculty has become more diversified in sex, race, and, not surprisingly, field of specialization. This increasing diversification has resulted from the dual commitments to the Little University concept and to an affirmative action recruiting policy.

Several changes in the student body are worth mentioning. First, the total enrollment of Wesleyan has risen from a little over 1,000 students in the late 1940s to the present 2,350. This gradual increase has resulted in conscious decisions to increase the amount of revenue derived from tuition and fees, thereby relieving deficits in the operating budget. Second, the students who are presently admitted are more diversified in race and sex than earlier Wesleyan students. In 1968 Wesleyan decided to reinstate a policy of coeducation, which it had abandoned in 1912. Further, the new African-American institute provides concrete evidence of Wesleyan's commitment to equality of educational opportunity for minorities. Wesleyan considers itself at the forefront of American colleges and universities, having established its minority recruitment program in 1965.

The academic ability of Wesleyan's students has remained high. Over the last decade, the percentage of entering freshmen graduating in the top 10 percent of their class has risen from 40 percent to 65 percent. And even though the average Scholastic Aptitude Test score of the entering class has been decreasing (a fact that Wesleyan ascribes to the nationwide decline in SAT scores), the average is approximately one standard deviation above the mean.

Wesleyan's RAMP Project

Wesleyan's RAMP proposal, submitted to the Exxon Education Foundation in 1972, indicated that the university was "not concerned about survival but about the continuing ability to lead." The threat to Wesleyan's leadership position resulted from five years of budget deficits. Primarily because of the large endowment, administrators and faculty alike historically perceived Wesleyan as a wealthy institution without limits to what it could do. Increasingly, however, they realized that there are definite limits on Wesleyan's fiscal resources.

The Threats to Wesleyan. A number of circumstances curtailed the enormous wealth of the institution. The continuing budget deficits began to eat into the endowment. Wesleyan consumed 8 to 9 percent of the market value of its endowment in the early 1970s. At that rate, the long-term strength of its endowment was seriously endangered. Further, the endowment assets were eroded by the general decline in the value of common stocks due to the recession in the mid 1970s. All this was coupled with a tremendous increase in operating costs (especially fuel costs) due to inflation. This combination of factors led Wesleyan to examine a variety of options to reduce and eliminate its operating deficits.

By way of background, Wesleyan followed the practice of preparing five- and ten-year projections of revenues and expenditures on a regular basis since the 1960s. Unfortunately, these long-range projections often proved quite different from the reality that followed. For instance, a 1964 projection had estimated that Wesleyan's expenditures would amount to approximately $11 million; they actually totaled $18 million. These inadequacies in Wesleyan's long-range projections led the university administrators to consider other strategies.

In 1972 the president appointed a committee to study measures to balance the budget by the middle of the 1970s. The alternative selected was to increase revenues by increasing enrollments from 1,800 students to 2,350 students and by implementing a tuition increase every other year. However, the unexpected increase in operating costs, particularly for fuel oil, and the economic recession, which had a disastrous effect on the performance of Wesleyan's portfolio, negated this solution. Although the university had increased its *income*, it was unable to control *"outgo" expenses*. Future attempts to balance the budget would require more stringent expenditure control, particularly with respect to the number of faculty and their salaries. One of the strategies selected to help control those costs was the installation of a management information system.

Selecting the SEARCH Model. In 1973 Wesleyan applied for a RAMP grant from the Exxon Foundation. Wesleyan selected the SEARCH model (described in Chapter Two) for its project. Although NCHEMS products and CAMPUS (also described in Chapter Two) were considered, SEARCH was selected mainly for its flexibility of program structure, terminology, and output reports. Wesleyan also owns several NCHEMS modules, but they have never been operationalized. A second reason for the adoption of SEARCH is the fact that Peat, Marwick, and Mitchell—the developers of the SEARCH model—were the auditors for the college and former employers of one vice-president and the project director. *Thus, in its search for an appropriate planning model, Wesleyan University looked first to a firm with whom it had had successful experiences.*

The SEARCH model is a "highly aggregated" computer simulation model developed especially for small private liberal arts colleges. The model consists of five modules: student, faculty, program, facilities, and finance. By "highly aggregated" we mean that data are collected for the first three modules at the level of colleges (such as arts and humanities) instead of departments. The facilities and financial modules are aggregated at a university-wide level. Each module contains three sets of variables: (1) *internal "current conditions" factors* (such as the level of student enrollment or the size of the faculty); (2) *"decision variables,"* factors that the institution can change (for example, the number of faculty, the level of student enrollment, the amount of faculty compensation, the rate of classroom usage, or the average classroom size); (3) *environmental "current situation"* variables, factors that are essentially outside the institution's control (for instance, rate of inflation, increases in fuel oil costs, or gifts from alumni).

The SEARCH model implemented by Wesleyan had several hundred of these "internal," "decision," and "environmental" variables. However, these variables can be reduced to ten basic factors that significantly influence Wesleyan's situation: student enrollments, faculty size, faculty salaries, research support, support services (such as secretarial or maintenance services), financial aid, inflation, endowment portfolio return, tuition rate, value of gifts and grants, capital expenditure, and debt service. In its attempts to control costs, Wesleyan gave particular attention to the decision variables regarding student/faculty ratio, faculty compensation, and student financial aid.

The SEARCH model helps establish relationships between these various factors. For instance, the student module may calculate the number of students who withdraw from the institution for a semester or more. At Wesleyan withdrawing students traditionally caused serious problems in estimating revenues from student tuition. The development of longitudinal data on these students led to better estimates of the total withdrawals from the university. As a result, the college has replaced its traditional pattern of underenrollment with a pattern of slight overenrollment. This was one example of how SEARCH data were used.

Applying the SEARCH Model to Decision Making

A primary financial objective of the Wesleyan administration was to reduce the percentage of endowment income used in current operating expenditures and to increase the pay-as-you-go portion based on tuition, fees, and other direct charges. Initially, only 45 percent of the operating expenditures came from the direct-income sources such as tuition. As of the 1977–78 fiscal year, the direct-income portion increased to 70 percent, with the final goal being 80 percent. In other words, the fundamental financial objective of Wesleyan was to reduce its reliance on the endowment income provided by its vast portfolio—and that was achieved. The story of *how* it was accomplished is interesting.

Shortly after the Exxon project was implemented, the president established an administrative task force to review the information from the SEARCH data, to study alternatives to balance the budget, and to design recommendations for decisions. The administration decided, in a widely criticized decision, *not* to form a faculty steering committee to consider the various options open to the institution. Instead, since the administration believed that decisions concerning program retrenchment could be made better by the central administration than by college faculty, the administration at Wesleyan issued a series of staff reports based heavily on data and projections from the SEARCH systems.

The first staff report, "On the Context for Planning and Decisions at Wesleyan," provided the background on the policy options available to the institution. Specific attention was given to the development of the "Little University" concept. Historical data were provided on the growth rate in student enrollment, college faculty, academic programs, and class size. The report ended with a review of Wesleyan's earlier attempts at long-range projection and an effort in 1972 to balance Wesleyan's financial situation. A second report gave supplemental information.

The third report, "Alternatives for Wesleyan," examined various courses of action that could be taken. This report covered areas of administration and physical plant, student and faculty levels, academic programs, admissions and financial aid, and institutional salary policies. In each of these areas, base projections were first made that assumed no changes; the current patterns were simply projected into the future. These base projections were then compared with a number of alternative courses of action. The question was this: "What if we did X or Y; how would it compare to the baseline, no-change projection?" For instance, the base projections about student enrollment first estimated the tuition income and financial aid expenses that would be involved in a no-change situation, maintaining an enrollment of 2,250 undergraduate students. These base projections were then compared with three alternatives: 2,350; 2,450; and 2,550. In the report the section on enrollment options concludes with a discussion of the constraints placed on enrollment increases—specifically those relating to physical facilities and the size of the institution's applicant pool. In this third "alternative" document, there was no attempt to *make decisions*. The purpose was to *lay out options* and to describe the real-world constraints on those options.

The final report, "A Plan for Action: 1975–1980," set forth the administration's recommendation for balancing the budget by the 1980 fiscal year. The final shoe was dropped; the alternatives were translated into decision recommendations. Most of the recommended decisions were oriented toward reducing *costs*, not raising new revenue. However, this orientation was not exclusive; a few alternatives for increasing revenues were also considered. This possibility of comparing institutional *expenditures* and *revenues* is one of the fundamental advantages of the SEARCH model.

Recommendations on Student/Faculty Ratios. In the first staff report, considerable attention was given to Wesleyan's student/faculty ratio, which was 10 to 1. Specifically, there were 2,350 students and 235 faculty. Of these 2,350 students, 2,250 were undergraduates and 100 were graduates. According to the first administration report, "It appears inevitable that the student/faculty ratio will have to increase."

In the third staff report, three different student/faculty ratios were considered: ratios of 11 to 1, 12 to 1, and 13 to 1. There are only two ways to increase a student/faculty ratio: by increasing the number of students or by decreasing the number of faculty. In arriving at a decision, Wesleyan projected various combinations of these two strategies. Increments of 100, 200, and 350 students were considered. By dividing each of these enrollment options by the various student/faculty ratios, the administrators could determine the decrease of faculty that would be required. After examining these alternatives, they concluded that "the financial impact of an increase in the student/faculty ratio, coupled with marked enrollment growth, is very substantial."

In the final "plan for action," the Wesleyan administrators decided to seek a student/faculty ratio between 12 to 1 and 13 to 1. The strategies essentially involved increasing the number of undergraduate students by 100. This enrollment increment was primarily to be composed of "special students," students who could enroll at Wesleyan on a part-time basis. An important consideration was that part-time students were not eligible for financial aid. In addition, Wesleyan decided to enlarge its second-semester student transfer program. Finally, it would admit a few additional full-time students in the fall semester. There were two basic reasons for limiting enrollment increases to 100: (1) facility constraints (that is, limitations in housing, dining room, academic, and library space) and (2) the size, composition, and quality of Wesleyan's applicant pool. The desired student/faculty ratio and the increment in student enrollment fixed the number of faculty reductions at forty positions, a substantial number in such a small university.

Two considerations figured prominently in the minds of the Wesleyan administrators as they made these recommendations. First, what impact would they have on the academic program? The administrators believed that a modest increase in the initially low student/faculty ratio would not hurt student-teacher relationships. Second, substantial consideration was given to the impact of these increases on tenure policies and practices. The administrators believed that the reduction of forty positions could be achieved by "orderly attrition"–through retirement, resignations, and death. They estimated that these reductions would amount to seventy positions in the four-year period projected. Consequently, faculty reductions would not, the administrators hoped, affect institutional policies or the morale of the junior faculty. Although they later found that the number of staff reductions through orderly attrition did not occur at the rate they had projected, this discrepancy was not substantial enough to destroy the plan to reduce Wesleyan's reliance on its endowment portfolio. In fact, this policy will result in net budget increases of $350,000 in 1979–80.

Recommendations on Faculty Salaries. The base rate projections of the first background report assumed that the faculty compensation would continue to increase at the annual historical rate of 7 percent. The administrators estimated that each percent increase required an additional expenditure of $100,000 in 1975–76. Further, these increases had a cumulative effect, since increases to the faculty salaries in one year constituted the salary base for additional faculty increases in subsequent years. Seven percent raises in 1974–75 would result in a cumulative expense of over $5 million in a six-year period. In the staff report "Alternatives for Wesleyan," three options to continued increases in faculty compensation were considered. The first was a one-year freeze in faculty compensation. This would result in an immediate savings of $700,000 for that fiscal year and an increasing cumulative effect later. Second, the institution could slow the growth in faculty compensation and thereby "significantly reduce projected expenditures." The administrators also considered reducing the level of fringe benefits; however, they concluded that fringe benefit reductions had "limited opportunities for cost savings."

In the final analysis, the university selected a reduction in the annual salary raises from 7 to 4 percent. Although this policy significantly reduced expenditures, the administrators realized that it would have a detrimental effect on faculty morale, would make the institution a less attractive place to work, and would make it more difficult to attract and retain faculty. However, a cost savings of $2.5 million outweighed these possible detrimental effects. In addition, it was unlikely that Wesleyan faculty could find other positions that would provide comparable compensation and work load. But it has proved more difficult to reduce the rate of growth of faculty compensation than the administrators anticipated. Because of numerous pressures, they are having to increase the rate of faculty compensation faster than the 4 percent planned.

Student Aid Recommendations. The final policy decision dealt with the student aid subsidy gap. It is well known that student-based financial aid programs are critical to a private institution's long-run financial viability. Over the last fifteen years, however, there has been an increasing gap between student aid expenditures and the revenues specifically designated for student aid programs. Student aid simply is not coming in as fast as it is going out. In fact, this gap has constituted one of the fastest-growing elements in the cost structure at many private colleges.

In 1974–75 Wesleyan had 725 students (approximately one third of its student body) on some form of financial aid.

Student aid cost the institution $1.9 million annually, but only $.7 million came from revenues specifically designated for that purpose. The difference, $1.2 million, had to be financed out of the institution's current funds. For Wesleyan, as well as a number of other private liberal arts colleges and universities, the dependence of student financial aid programs on current operating monies could not be allowed to continue.

Wesleyan considered three alternatives to its current financial aid policies. First, it could maintain the current situation, in effect letting the student applicant pool decide the amount of financial expenditures by the institution. However, this blind admissions strategy was risky. There was no guarantee that the percentage of students needing financial aid might not rise. Second, it could maintain its current financial aid policy but restructure the self-help component of its aid program. Currently, Wesleyan expected that its students would provide at least $1,400 toward the cost of attending. Any restructuring would have to take into account Wesleyan's competitive position with other prestigious liberal arts institutions in the Northeast. Third, Wesleyan could change its admissions policies—either by including economic criteria in the selection process or by limiting financial aid awards to a small group of students.

Although the final policy combined all three options, it basically represents a continuation of Wesleyan's "blind admissions" program. This decision is primarily the result of pressure from the student body. However, the administrators also decided not to exceed the current $1.2 million for the student aid program. Through a combination of increasing income and decreasing expenses, they felt that current financial aid programs could be maintained without increases in the current fund expenditures. Finally, they decided to restrict admissions of foreign students to those who could pay. This restriction was combined with an increase in the number of part-time students—who were not eligible for aid. Taken together, these policies meant that there would be only a slight increase ($87,000) in the money spent on financial aid. These practices would be reviewed annually, so that financial aid expenditures could be closely monitored.

A Successful Project?

In the final report to the Exxon Foundation, Wesleyan University concluded: "On the basis of the experience of the past three years, it is fair to say that the SEARCH model has been successfully integrated into the Wesleyan planning and budgeting process. It has proven its worth as a significant analytical tool on a continuing basis." Three of the four administrators responding to a follow-up questionnaire indicated that the SEARCH model had become "a fundamental part of the college management process." All these administrators indicated that long-range planning of the institution had improved because of the Exxon project.

It must be emphasized that SEARCH is only a means to an end; it is only the information source for a larger planning effort. As the associate treasurer indicated, "The emphasis has been on problems and solutions and not on the systems themselves. We are highly sensitive to process, particularly the participatory process." The four reports produced by the Wesleyan administration apparently were fairly successful in disseminating information to various members of the campus constituency. The *entire process* of analyzing information, defining alternatives, and consulting with various constituencies was connected to the SEARCH data base in a holistic planning effort. It was *not* the data system alone; it was the entire planning cycle that made Wesleyan's program effective.

The services provided by the consulting firm significantly contributed to the project's success. There are two components to this contribution: the familiarity between the consulting firm and the administration, and the types of services provided. Peat, Marwick, and Mitchell had a long history of service to the institution. As the external auditing firm, they were already very knowledgeable about the institution and its needs. Undoubtedly, this knowledge and sophistication facilitated the efforts of the consulting firm to adapt the SEARCH model to Wesleyan's *unique* needs, an adaptation that often did not occur at less fortunate institutions. In addition, two of the top administrators at Wesleyan had been former employees of the consulting firm. These personal relationships undoubtedly helped pave the way for a fruitful consulting relationship.

Foremost among the services provided by the consulting firm was the retraining of Wesleyan administrators so that they could maintain the software after the project's end. Fortunately, the administration and the consultants shared a desire to train several people. Subsequent staff turnover easily might have killed the project if replacements had not been available. In the long run, retraining existing personnel is probably the most important service that can be provided by a consulting firm. Unfortunately, this retraining was not provided by all the other various consulting firms retained by Exxon grant institutions. And in some cases only one person was trained, leaving the institution highly vulnerable to disruption in the event of staff turnover.

In addition, it seems that Wesleyan's organizational development strategy—the wide dissemination and discussion of the four staff reports in order to achieve a broad participatory process—was moderately successful. This strategy is unique among the various projects. Needless to say, not everyone agreed that the reports, prepared and controlled by the administration, provided the best framework for making such crucial decisions. Some fairly strong faculty criticism of the program emerged. A number of people were critical of the form of the administrative reports and the lack of faculty input to the decisions. In our on-campus interviews, several people made negative comments. One senior professor, for example, said: "This procedure—publishing those staff reports—is a problem. I recognize the administration's problem. Fast action is needed, and Lord only knows that faculty take forever. And the administration has the real information on which decisions have to be made. But—and here's the rub—this is a high-quality faculty with a rich history of self-governance and participation. And this administratively dominated process flies in the face of the institution's deep-rooted history. I see the administration's dilemma, but I wish they'd been more sensitive to people's feelings and the institution's heritage."

Each report was disseminated to all members of the campus community who wished to be involved, and open discussions were held, so that faculty and students would be allowed to express their opinions. But many people felt that the discussion was much too short. Generally, members of the campus community had approximately two to three weeks to discuss the various reports as they were issued. After this time the administration presented the staff report to the board of trustees for their comment and/or approval. For the final report the faculty had approximately six weeks to discuss the plan that had been developed by the university's administration. One disgruntled faculty member said, "The discussion was definitely short-cut. A few weeks to discuss the fate of the university—ridiculous!" But one administrator retorted: "The entire process took a whole year! And still people said it was short-circuited. Listen, if we'd had a decade of discussion some dispirited professor would scream it had been crammed down his throat."

During this period of financial crisis, the faculty at Wesleyan, like the faculty at many less wealthy institutions, apparently became isolated from the administration. The lack of academic backgrounds among college administrators often causes the faculty to question their ability to make decisions based on educational rather than financial criteria. A typical comment was this: "The president doesn't really seem to understand what faculty members are all about—having never been one himself." This growing alienation resulted in a number of faculty actions. Initially the faculty voted to dissolve the university senate—which had been composed of many campus groups, including students and administrators—and to eliminate parity between faculty and students on the Educational Policy Committee. The faculty may have felt that such action was necessary to provide Wesleyan with the academic leadership that was missing or to protect their salaries and academic programs from the pressure of a tight cost control policy.

Still, the faculty were somewhat hopeful. The campus was by no means totally split, nor was the faculty morale really that bad. They generally felt that they had "adequate opportunity" for input into the college administration, although it is questionable whether such input had any impact. Further, the faculty felt that the president was "a great improvement as president" in that he was "always available for consultation and discussions." Perhaps the negative feelings directed at the staff report procedure were only minor ripples of discontent. Certainly the facul-

ty did not uniformly fight the decisions. In fact, in this time of
crisis for higher education, Wesleyan's faculty (compared to the
faculty at other colleges) seem to have taken the admittedly minor adjustments in stride.

Lessons to Be Learned

The single most important lesson to be learned from Wesleyan's experience, in terms of the long-run financial viability of
private liberal arts colleges, is the importance of assessing and
balancing growth rates of various revenues and expenditures. Initially, Wesleyan attempted a revenues-oriented solution to its deficit problem; it soon realized, however, that "strict expenditure
control policies" also had to be implemented. Thus, in order to
assess the implications of various fiscal policies, one must assess
the impact of these policies on both income and expenditures.

Further, *balancing* revenues and expenditures at any particular time is only one piece of a complex financial puzzle. In
addition to balancing a budget (or, in Wesleyan's case, reducing
reliance on an endowment portfolio), institutions must analyze
the growth rate in various categories of revenues and expenditures; that is, study *future trends* and *long-term* effects. Wesleyan found, for example, that slowing the growth in faculty salaries had a substantial long-term financial effect. In the long run,
private liberal arts colleges must achieve parity not only in the
current situation but also in the future *incremental changes* in
revenues and expenditures.

Long-run financial equilibrium depends largely on planning
—for instance, on identifying critical decision variables that substantially affect the financial viability of the college. According
to the project director, "The considerable emphasis upon planning and budgeting at Wesleyan over the last six years has produced another important benefit. Those *few critical variables* in
each aspect of the university's operations which can vitally influence plans have gradually been identified. These variables are
monitored regularly in such areas as staffing, enrollments, financial aid, fund-raising, and energy."

A second aspect of institutional planning is implementation, for plans are no better than the real-world action based on
them. At Wesleyan staff reports were designed to facilitate broad

participation and information exchange among members of various campus constituencies. Apparently, this strategy was successful, even though it had a few critics. To be successful, organizational development strategies and plans must be consistent with the climate, history, and heritage of the institution. Apparently the periodic staff reports at Wesleyan helped communicate to the campus community vital information and data, and in turn the feedback was used in the decisions.

It is important to see the MIS program at Wesleyan in its total context as one small piece of an overall planning strategy. The process is far more than just a computer churning out pages of data. It is also important to note the relationship between *long-range* planning and the *annual* budget process. Again quoting the project director, "The five-year plan is the overall context for the annual budget cycle. It is a reference point for consideration of the immediate and longer-term consequences of decisions made concerning rates of faculty salary increase, program development, and staff additions." It is critical to assess the *long-term* financial impact of these decisions. The future consequences of present decisions have to be assessed. It is this future-oriented decision making that distinguishes a really sophisticated effort at managerial improvement.

Finally, Wesleyan's experience with its consulting firm demonstrates that such a firm can be very useful in the implementation of these projects. Three factors helped in Wesleyan's situation: (1) familiarity of the consulting firm with the institution, (2) familiarity of the institution with the consulting firm, and (3) training of institutional staff. It is important, if not ethically imperative, that consulting firms develop substantial expertise in the operations of their clients. To simply apply routine solutions to an institution's problems precipitates failure in the project and institutional ill will toward the outside consultants. Alternatively, the institutions themselves must develop a familiarity with the consulting firms and their products. This will allow institutions to identify products that actually meet their needs and will subsequently enable the institution to carry its end of the responsibility in the dual partnership between consultant and campus. Finally, consulting firms should, at the very least, train several college personnel, so that the institution will be able to maintain their project after the consultants leave. The implications of the failure to provide such training have been demonstrated repeatedly among Exxon grant recipients. Fortunately, Wesleyan and its consultants adequately did their background work so that the project could be successfully implemented.

Using Resource Allocation Models

Founded in 1896, Clarkson College of Technology is a private, independent, coeducational institution located in Potsdam, New York. The original class of seventeen students has grown to a 1979 enrollment of 2,500 students. The college is essentially a residential campus, with on-campus housing for approximately 2,000 students.

Clarkson's major organizational units are the School of Arts and Sciences, the School of Engineering, the School of Management, the Graduate School, and the Division of Research. While the curriculum emphasizes the pure and applied sciences, programs in management, the humanities, and the social sciences are also offered. Advanced degrees at the master's and/or doctoral level are offered in engineering, management, and the physical sciences. Clarkson, as a member of the Associated Colleges of the St. Lawrence Valley Consortium, has ready access to most resources of the three other college members. Cooperative academic programs, joint cultural and social events, and shared faculty and computer resources have been a significant asset to Clarkson.

The college employs 175 full-time faculty (56 percent of them tenured), maintaining a student/faculty ratio of about 14 to 1. Clarkson faculty members serve both undergraduate and graduate programs. Individual scholarship in research, along with teaching, is emphasized as part of the faculty member's responsibility.

As would be expected from a technological college, Clarkson students are generally of high ability, particularly in the areas of mathematics and mechanical abilities. Over 40 percent of its students have a high school grade point average of A or A-, as compared with the 21 percent national average for four-year institutions. Eighty-five percent of the students are New York State residents, and they tend to come from families only slightly more affluent than students nationally. The major distinction between Clarkson students and those at other four-year institutions is their emphasis on engineering careers. Sixty-four percent, as compared with 5 percent of the students nationally, are oriented toward engineering.

In response to the rapid enrollment growth over the 1948–1968 period, both the physical plant and staffing were expanded. However, this expansion in enrollment was reversed in the four-year period from 1968 to 1972. To quote from the Clarkson Exxon proposal, "To maintain our present full-time-equivalent total enrollment, the new entering freshman class must number 630 for two successive years, which is 160 more than the new freshman enrollment in the fall of 1972." In the same four years, Clarkson's dependence on tuitions as its primary revenue source grew from 68 to 75 percent. As the college was becoming more dependent on student tuitions and fees, the costs of its operation were growing. For instance, educational and general expenditures per student credit hour increased slightly over 6 percent per year during this period. These two factors, combined with a number of others, led Clarkson College to seek improved resource allocation procedures. While such procedures and programs "will not give answers to all the problems facing the small, private, specialized college, they can provide the basis for a strong, rigorous, rational strategy to dampen losses in adverse times. And they can magnify the gains in prosperous times."

Project Implementation

Perhaps because of the engineering-management-science environment at Clarkson, there has been considerable interest in developing and maintaining a data base useful for management decision making. As early as 1970, Clarkson manually undertook a study to determine the unit cost of instruction per student by level and discipline. The following year, a resource model was implemented as part of a pilot study with NCHEMS. Unfortunately, plans to expand the program were sharply curtailed. At that time the college had suffered from low freshman enrollments for two consecutive years and was in a difficult financial situation. It decided not to deploy limited resources into this area. In retrospect, however, several administrators indicated that this was an unwise decision. Actually, the more precarious an institution's fiscal condition, the greater the need for a thorough understanding of revenues and costs. Therefore, in 1973 Clarkson applied for and received a grant from the Exxon Education Foundation to resume development of a resource allocation program.

Goals and Expected Outcomes of the Resource Allocation Program. The Resource Allocation Management Program (RAMP) that finally emerged was designed to (1) identify and list actual or projected resources (inputs) available to the institution; (2) identify the type and source of institutional costs (outputs); (3) define the relationship between inputs and outputs; (4) facilitate the use of predetermined decision criteria (cost effectiveness) to arrive at resource allocation decisions.

Although Clarkson had experienced a moderate financial crunch in 1971–72, implementation of RAMP was not in response to a financial panic; rather, it was considered a way to improve institutional decision making about resource use. The administrators believed that a resource allocation program would help them evaluate decision alternatives realistically and consistently. By the use of sophisticated quantitative analytical tools and models, the president felt that important variables affecting the institution's future could be identified, numerically expressed, and related mathematically in ways that approximate reality. Thus, the resource allocation process became directly linked to overall institutional planning.

Selection of a Task Force. A task force, representing various college divisions, was selected. Membership included the college president, the dean of the graduate school, the director of research, the controller and assistant treasurer, the associate dean of students, the director of institutional planning, the director of undergraduate financial aid, four faculty members (selected from the faculty senate), and two students. This task force was to serve two functions: (1) to educate and obtain support and insight from faculty and staff through a series of discussions and review sessions during the experimental program; (2) to review the existing data base and programs prior to the selection of a final series of automated programs. Clarkson recognized quite early that the need for complete, accessible, and compatible information justified the time and expense involved in the redesign of its data-collection procedures. Fortunately, it is a one-time expense; once the college has made all data compatible, their maintenance is no more expensive than in the old form. Without an integrated information system to feed the cost analysis program, college personnel must manually feed the data necessary to drive the resource allocation programs. This takes considerable time and effort. With an integrated system, the data are more readily available.

Selection and Use of Resource Allocation Models

After the *data base* had been carefully revised, Clarkson began to use new *software* to make financial decisions about resource allocations. A number of alternative software programs were available. The college considered three basic alternatives: SEARCH, CAMPUS, and NCHEMS (see Chapter Two). NCHEMS' Costing and Data Management System (CADMS) was chosen for four reasons: (1) "It was more economical." (2) "It provided for continuity" in the development of the college's management information system. (3) It would be the most "compatible with future demands of national, state, and private agencies." (4) Although it demanded common definitions and procedures for interinstitutional exchanges, it still could be modified to fit the decision requirements of the institution.

Largely due to the painstaking efforts of the task force, Clarkson has developed a very sophisticated computer-based information system. How Clarkson elaborated on the basic logic of resource allocation models will now be described.

Enrollment Projections. As a private college with limited endowment funds, Clarkson's resource base is largely dependent on the student enrollment size. Many factors affect enrollments, some of which are difficult to quantify. An enrollment projection model was developed that would determine (1) a projection of the full-time-equivalent enrollment, which could estimate tuition income and state aid under the New York State "Bundy Plan"; (2) the number of faculty required; and (3) the housing needs for single and married students by year.

Projections were made for entering freshmen. They were based on the number of in-state and out-of-state high school graduates, transfer students, and the retention of continuing students. To provide an idea of the complexity of these projections, Clarkson estimated the number of students from within the state on the basis of Clarkson's ability to attract students, the rate of growth in high school students, and the college-going rate of these students, all by geographical region. Currently, Clarkson has projected enrollments through 1985.

Student Flow Models. Clarkson is able to convert these enrollment projections into probable student majors. Further, the college charts changes in student major from matriculation through graduation withdrawal. For instance, Clarkson has traced the 112 undecided majors who matriculated in the fall of 1971 to the 94 who remained in the fall of 1973. Further, those 94 students were distributed among a number of possible majors. As indicated in Chapter Two, the number of student majors (by level) is the essential element for converting the Induced Course Load Matrix (ICLM) into the Induced Work Load Matrix (IWLM). Clarkson also found the ICLM useful for several management purposes in addition to cost analysis. ICLM data were used to study the implications of possible steady-state enrollments in various departments. The program was also used to predict the effects of changing the course curriculum of a given major and of eliminating or adding a major.

While using these data, Clarkson discovered that many previous assumptions about the degree of departmental interdependence could no longer be supported by quantitative data. For example, Clarkson frequently had made decisions based on the assumption that the chemistry and physics graduate programs were closely interrelated; actual data, however, revealed that graduate students in one department took no course work in the other.

Faculty-Need Projections. Once the IWLM is obtained, the number of faculty for each department is estimated. This estimation additionally requires the establishment of institutional policies concerning the student/faculty ratios. In addition, Clarkson is able to estimate how future faculty size, composition, and salaries will be affected by policy changes in hiring, retirements, promotions, and the like. Some of the options considered by Clarkson included the following: (1) Change the tenure policy to giving no credit toward tenure for previous experience at another institution. (2) Change the annual inflation factor from 4 to 5 percent. (3) Change the distribution of new hires to include 20 percent instructors and 57 percent assistants.

Resource Requirements Prediction Model (RRPM). The Resource Requirements Prediction Model is intended to estimate the direct instructional cost per student, by type of program and level, and the allocated full instructional cost per student. In 1970 Clarkson began using this model. While the program was designed primarily for prediction, it can also be used for computing and analyzing current costs. The program included data from the Induced Course Load Matrix, the Induced Work Load Matrix, a faculty data module, and a costing module.

Although Clarkson chose to use the Costing and Data Management System (CADMS), it continued to use RRPM because this model was, in certain respects, more suitable to the institution's needs. Clarkson is a relatively small college where individual faculty and administrative assignments are not complex. A comprehensive method such as CADMS was too complex and time-consuming to warrant extended use. Moreover, RRPM was less expensive to run and easier to understand, the implementation demands were well within the reach of a modest computer capability and staff resources, and it could answer "what-if" questions.

Revenue Analysis. Standard CADMS software does not enable users to analyze the revenues generated by the various disciplines and student majors. Using a self-generated module on CADMS, Clarkson distributed operational revenue to the various academic programs—"directly as it was earned or allocated, in the same manner as the associated costs were allocated" to the academic departments. According to Clarkson, "no analysis improved the old resource allocation process more than this revenue-cost program."

With this revenue analysis program, Clarkson was able to determine the amount of unsupported operational costs for each academic program and for each major. For instance, the unsupported operational costs for graduate students majoring in civil and environmental engineering were estimated to be $159 per student credit hour, or $3,186 per full-time-equivalent student. This latter figure is roughly the difference between the estimated full cost per full-time graduate student in civil and environmental engineering ($5,757) and the tuition charged these students ($2,625). These unsupported costs had to be made up by such nonoperational revenues as endowments, gifts and grants, and earned interest income.

Applying the Resource Allocation Models to Decision Making

The primary objective of Clarkson's project was to improve financial allocations. Information produced by the cost analysis programs was used in several ways by the Clarkson management. Perhaps one of the most important decisions based on these programs was to increase the student/faculty ratio to 18 to 1. As indicated earlier, Clarkson had suffered two years of enrollment declines. These declines had resulted in severe financial pressure on the institution, because of increased unit costs of instructional programs and lost tuition revenues. Consequently, when enrollments began to increase, the decision was made to hold the number of faculty constant, thus increasing the student/faculty ratio. An immediate consequence of this decision was a reduction in the unit direct costs of Clarkson's academic program. In a personal conversation, a college administrator stated that this decision to increase the student/faculty ratio was based on long-term financial implications. Further, the information on these financial implications was produced by the institution's software. This information included anticipated reductions in the unit direct costs and increases in total revenues derived from student tuition and fees. Thus, the information produced by these packages influenced the decision to alter this fundamental instructional program policy.

Besides increasing the student/faculty ratio, Clarkson established other policies resulting from information provided by its various planning models. These policies included (1) setting tenure limits by school (based on the internally developed faculty-need projection model), (2) establishing tentative steady-state plans (based on its internally developed student flow model), and (3) increasing food and dormitory charges (due to a revenue-cost analysis of auxiliary enterprises). Overall, 90 percent of the administrators queried indicated that institutional forecasts and long-range planning had changed for the better as a result of the resource allocation program.

Another critical issue was the decision to retain the graduate program in the department of physics instead of combining the graduate program of the physics and chemistry departments. The core of this decision was information produced by the Induced Course Load Matrix. The ICLM showed no graduate student in either department taking a course in the other department. Thus, the costs per student major indicate that there would be no substantial savings if the two programs were collapsed.

Information produced by CADMS can be used for management purposes other than cost analysis. One such purpose is building legitimacy with faculty. For instance, the research faculty at Clarkson felt that the salary recovery rates at Clarkson were greater than the cost incurred by the college. Based on the data, however, this was not the case. Data are also used by such groups as the Faculty Committee on Academic Standards. The analysis of the Induced Course Load Matrix data allows this committee to ascertain the mix of the level of courses taken by majors in different departments. This analysis helps the Academic Standards Committee evaluate programs of majors in different departments. Most important of all is the fact that budgets are based on this project. The college's ability to attach income to cost is especially important in preparing these budgets. This comparison of revenues and expenditures identifies academic units which have a high level of unsupported operational costs. These unsupported costs could lead the institution to consider a policy of variable tuition rates, although such a policy has not yet been instituted. At the very least, this ability provides the institution with a real measure of dollar resource allocation.

A Successful Project?

Interviews and questionnaire data indicated substantial agreement among administrators that the various software programs had become an integral part of college management. More important, resource allocation to academic departments has been much improved. Over 75 percent of the administrators reported that the new budgeting and staffing procedures had resulted in more efficient management. Consequently, if one were to ask a Clarkson administrator today whether the two-year resource allocation project was worth the effort in resources expended, the answer would probably be an emphatic "yes." As one Clarkson administrator indicated, "If you consider only the dollar investment versus the dollar return, it would be easy to demonstrate that in the first year we recovered our initial investment; in the second year we recovered an amount equal to the entire Exxon grant plus our investment."

The entire Clarkson staff deemed the project moderately to very successful. A general opinion that "We have really only touched the surface in utilizing these programs" was expressed by several administrators. It was anticipated that, as familiarity with the programs increased, so would their use. Many of those interviewed also responded that they could foresee potential uses for the program having little to do with dollars. One illustration would be the use of systematic information and forecast by academic committees in curriculum planning and program adjustment. Future student academic interests and needs could be met in this way.

In short, the time, cost, and effort expended were not excessive compared to the benefits derived. The cost of developing a resource allocation program will vary widely with each college according to the program required, the state of the data files, the computer hardware available, and technical expertise. In retrospect, college administrators seem to agree that, even in a stringent financial atmosphere, a college is wise to divert some of its resources to such a program. Using its own resources, Clarkson did develop an RRPM several years prior to receiving the Exxon grant. However, the additional Exxon funds permitted an intensified effort. Clarkson's experience suggests that the costs are largely developmental. Clarkson expects to continue its present level of operation with an additional budget cost of about $2,000. Through our on-campus interviews and analyses of questionnaires, we were able to nail down a few specific areas of improvement that resulted from RAMP projects.

1. *The college information system became more accessible, accurate, and complete.* Clearly, Clarkson needed to develop a system capable of supplying all the essential raw data to the various programs. However, these data needed to be aggregated, interpreted, and appropriately conveyed. Clarkson was fortunate to have accurate and rather extensive data files. The organization of the files, however, normally did not permit multiple uses and flexibility. To illustrate, proper records were maintained concerning currently enrolled student's name, address, major, accumulated academic credits, grade point average, and current enrollment status. But these data were not sufficient to project, for example, the future upper-class distribution of current freshmen, the academic load for various departments, or the on-campus housing needs for the next decade. The same situation prevailed in the accounting system. Clarkson's accounting system was designed primarily to identify and record income and expenditure transactions accurately and to control against overspending. Although the system contained vast amounts of transaction data, in their present form they were relatively inaccessible and useless for cost analysis purposes.

According to questionnaire data and interviews, most Clarkson administrators (90 percent) felt that the overall quality of the institutional information system had improved. Not only were data more accurate and accessible, but they were presented in a more timely manner and a more useful form. All agreed that data concerning faculty had improved immensely, and 85 percent felt that the quality of student information had improved. There was less consensus about the college financial data. While 75 percent of these administrators cited improvement in the overall quality of financial data, half indicated that the availability and timeliness of the information had not changed appreciably.

2. *The implementation of RAMP increased awareness among the various campus constituencies.* Access to information

is important for understanding the complexities of the modern university or college. RAMP provided the total college community with a broader, more realistic perspective about the institution— its goals, its resource use, and its ultimate survival in an environment of enrollment stability. Despite the faculty's acceptance of RAMP, faculty participation in resource allocation decisions does not seem to have increased. Although the process of implementing the project was open, resource allocation has apparently remained highly centralized in the administrative sector. Only 9 percent of the questionnaire respondents indicated that these decisions have become more decentralized to the departmental level.

3. *The resource allocation program proved to be a valuable tool for interinstitutional comparisons.* Toward the conclusion of RAMP, Clarkson participated in a comparison between itself and Worcester Polytechnic Institute, another private engineering and science–oriented college. The objective was to obtain comparative costs for similar programs. Clarkson benefited from the review. It prompted further study of the operation of auxiliary enterprises as well as research. Coupled with revenue-cost analyses, it stimulated some policy changes. In a similar manner, WPI was able to identify areas of difference. These areas indicated a need for further study on its part.

Lessons to Be Learned

Although no college can produce a financial management program applicable to another college, certain lessons that emerged from the Clarkson experience can be shared by most small private colleges.

1. *Accurate and complete data are essential.* Arguments against the development of an extensive data base always cite the expense involved in data collection. It was Clarkson's experience that all the essential data already existed; the real task was to make them available in a compatible form, by reorganizing data files and controlling data definitions.

2. *Multiple programs are necessary.* Clarkson found that no single automated program could produce the information required for a comprehensive program. Instead, a series of well-

chosen, well-understood, and carefully linked subsystems were necessary to produce proper data and corresponding analyses.

3. *The operation and management of data handling should be identified as a formal organizational unit of the college.* Resource allocation is a continuous process at Clarkson. Data collection and information analysis from various internal and external sources are critical to the program's total functioning. These functions can be most efficiently performed and coordinated if the data-handling unit is identified as a separate entity with an adequate professional support staff.

4. *A capable director-manager of the data-handling unit is needed.* Both the implementation and the continued maintenance of a resource allocation program require a competent, professional, and able manager who understands its objectives. Clarkson attributes much of the success in its program development, as well as its subsequent modification, to the expertise, professional judgment, and continuity provided by the director. The degree of trust placed in this director was manifested in the administrative reorganization. The project director became the assistant to the president for institutional planning. Such administrative reorganization has occurred at a number of other Exxon grant institutions. Despite the importance of this trust, the project should not be a one-man show. The various programs must be widely understood, and staff must be trained in the use of the program. Failure to provide such training has resulted in the demise of many Exxon projects due to staff turnover.

5. *Top administrative involvement is essential.* The chief executive officer must endorse the program in spirit as well as in actions. At Clarkson this dedication was evident from the project's inception. Only after the president made it clear to the total college staff that the program would indeed be used in management decision making, however, did the program activity receive a dynamic role in the college. Ninety percent of the questionnaire respondents indicated that the top administration was fully supportive of this effort. However, only 54 percent perceived a heavy involvement in the actual process.

6. *College-wide participation in program development and implementation is prudent and necessary.* Clarkson chose to

use a task force to include faculty and students in designing its program. However, it is not clear whether involvement remained widespread subsequent to program implementation. Perceptions about faculty attitudes toward the project indicate that relatively few (18 percent of the respondents) felt faculty to be strongly supportive; 63 percent indicated moderate faculty support. In practice, faculty involvement in internal decisions is quite limited. Not only is there little involvement; there is apparently little concern on the part of faculty. Perhaps due to the engineering-oriented environment of the college, faculty are less resistant to decisions being based on "numbers."

7. *Resource allocation requires judgmental decisions, many of which are political.* Critics of more rational approaches to management will argue that decisions always end up intuitively or politically based. Given this apparent fact of life, the development of sophisticated quantitative systems can hardly be justified. Although the administrators at Clarkson would agree that resource allocation analyses can only assist in making decisions, they emphatically believe that quantitative information is still a necessary tool. They would also insist that, even though every institution has its political realities, these realities should not become the sole dictator of decision making. They therefore concluded that political considerations, like quality considerations, must remain one of the many judgmental, unquantifiable components which policymakers use along with data analyses to make management decisions.

8. *Revenue analyses are essential to resource allocation decisions.* As will be emphasized in a later chapter, the long-run financial health of private liberal arts colleges is dependent on balancing the growth rates of institutional revenues and expenditures. Unfortunately, most programs focus on expenditures. Clarkson recognized that this is clearly insufficient for the analysis of internal resource allocation procedures. Thus, it expended energy in developing a procedure for analyzing institutional revenues as well. This ability to compare institutional revenues and expenditures is a *critical* component in the institution's long-run financial viability.

Chapter Four

Understanding Management by Objectives

In the early stages of the Resource Allocation Management Program (RAMP), almost all the institutions developed management information systems (MIS). Later, however, the Exxon Education Foundation funded some institutions that proposed management by objectives (MBO) projects. In every case the MBO project was established in conjunction with an MIS, so that the resulting system was a *combination* of projects. However, since we have discussed MIS activities at length in previous chapters, we will concentrate almost exclusively on the MBO side of these combination projects.

General Principles of MBO

The term *management by objectives* was probably first used by Peter Drucker (1954) in his *Practice of Management*.

However, probably the best-known discussion of the technique is George S. Odiorne's (1965) *Management by Objectives*. Many different activities occur under the general rubric of management by objectives. There are almost as many versions of MBO as there are people who talk about the issue. Nevertheless, it is probably safe to say that Odiorne's discussion is the most widely accepted version, and we will focus for a moment on his definitions.

What is a management by objectives system? Odiorne (pp. 55, 56, vii, viii) summarizes the approach in these words:

> In brief, the system of management by objectives can be described as a process whereby the superior and subordinate managers of an organization jointly identify its common goals, define each individual's major areas of responsibility in terms of the results expected of him, and use these measures as guides for operating the unit and assessing the contribution of each of its members.
>
> The primary effects of operating by management by objectives are to be seen in such tangible results as improved profit, more growth, lower costs, and increased revenues. On a more intangible plane, it also makes bureaucracy less tenable by affecting such secondary variables as production, quality, housekeeping, sales volume, staff work, and research effectiveness. Its tertiary effects are visible in such areas as better morale, more promotable people, improved quality of service, and improved delegation of decision making.
>
> The major premises of management by objectives can be stated as follows:
>
> A. Business management takes place within an economic system that provides the environmental situation for the individual firm. This environment, which has changed drastically over the past 30 years, imposes new requirements on companies and on individual managers.
>
> B. Management by objectives is a way of managing aimed at meeting these new requirements. It

presumes that the first step in management is to identify, by one means or another, the goals of the organization. All other management methods and subsystems follow this preliminary step.

C. Once organizational goals have been identified, orderly procedures for distributing responsibilities among individual managers are set up in such a way that their combined efforts are directed toward achieving those goals.

D. Management by objectives assumes that managerial behavior is more important than manager personality, and that this behavior should be defined in terms of results measured against established goals, rather than in terms of common goals for all managers, or common methods of managing.

E. It also presumes that while participation is highly desirable in goal setting and decision making, its principal merit lies in social and political values rather than its effects on production, though even here it may have a favorable impact, and in any case seldom hurts.

F. It regards the successful manager as a manager of situations, most of which are best defined by identifying the purpose of the organization and the managerial behavior best calculated to achieve that purpose.

It is obvious from Odiorne's discussion that MBO is basically a *planning process*, in which goals are set, tasks assigned to people throughout the organization, and evaluations made in light of goal achievement. Of course, setting goals and assigning tasks were key functions for managers long before the MBO process was conceived. However, the proponents of MBO argue that it offers a more structured and systematic method for planning and appraising performance. In effect, MBO is a systematic and careful procedure for activities that managers have always performed in looser form.

Odiorne (1965, pp. 70–73) has outlined the basic processes for establishing a management by objectives system. These are his key steps:

Step one. Identify the common goals of the whole organizational unit for the coming period. This is based on your desired goals for the whole organization, which are stated in terms of the measures of organization performance you intend to apply at the end of the period.

Step two. Clarify your working organization chart. Sketch the actual organization of the group under your supervision, showing titles, duties, relationships, and impending changes.

Step three. Set objectives for the next budget year with each man individually. Here's how you go about this:

a. Ask the subordinate to make notes on what objectives *he* has in mind for next year.

b. Before the meeting, list some objectives you'd like to see him include for the next year and have them ready.

c. In your personal conference, review the man's own objectives in detail, then offer your own suggestions or changes.

d. Have two copies of the final draft of his objectives typed; give him one and keep one yourself.

e. Working from the final agreement, ask him what *you* can do to help him accomplish his targets. Note his suggestions, keep them with your copy, and include them in your objectives, if pertinent.

Step four. During the year check each subordinate's goals as promised milestones are reached:

a. Is he meeting his target?

b. Are you delivering on your part in helping him?

c. Use the jointly agreed-upon goals as a tool for coaching, developing, and improving each man's performance on a continuous basis. Reinforce good results by feedback of *success* when you see it.

Step five. Near the end of the budget year, ask each subordinate to prepare a brief "statement of performance against budget," using his copy of his performance budget as a guide.

Step six. Set a date to go over this report in detail. Search for causes of variances.

Step seven. At this meeting, also, you can cover other things that may be on his mind. If he's so disposed, you might discuss such matters as relationships on the job, opportunity, job-related personal problems, and so on.

Step eight. Set the stage for establishing the subordinate's performance budget for the coming year. Here, of course, the manager finds himself back at Step one of the goal-setting stage, but better equipped by reason of his experience to set more realistic goals for the next budget period.

From this discussion, it is clear that the management by objectives process has some critical elements. First, it is an important *planning procedure*, by which goals and objectives for the organization are set on an annual basis. Second, Odiorne frequently mentions the importance of *linking the planning and the budgeting cycles*, so that budgets are clearly understood as instruments for achieving organizational goals. Third, the MBO process allows the *assignment of tasks and responsibilities* to people in the organization. Fourth, the procedure provides for systematic *evaluation* of people's performances. A worker's achievements can be compared with the original objectives to identify areas for improvement.

What experience did the Exxon RAMP institutions have with MBO? As we mentioned, no Exxon institution implemented a program that was strictly management by objectives. Instead, they all combined an MBO process with a management information system. Moreover, none of the institutions adapted the strategy to its unique needs. No two projects were alike, nor did any of them correspond exactly to Odiorne's description.

Most projects implemented by Exxon institutions were essentially *planning* enterprises. The other elements of a full-blown MBO project, especially the evaluation of employees by comparing their achievements with their stated goals, were either omitted or downplayed. In many ways our research staff felt that the projects conducted in the Exxon institutions would have been better named "planning strategies." But the institutions themselves proclaimed that they were implementing MBO projects. We have accepted their terminology, even though we have reservations about whether these were full-blown MBO systems.

Impact of MBO Projects

Let us now examine some general impacts that the research team felt were common to all the successful MBO projects. The following conclusions were derived from our interviews, questionnaires, and site evaluations on many campuses.

1. *Planning became a focused, systematic, college-wide process.* Most of the individuals interviewed indicated that there was a greater institutional focus on planning since the projects had been initiated. As one respondent said, "The MBO program helped us avoid the 'drift' we were experiencing before." The planning process, as developed in most institutions, was more comprehensive and participatory than the procedures used before the project began. The entire planning cycle usually took a year. Each cycle involved goal setting, budget making, and evaluation. College-wide participation was often effective in creating a willingness to plan and to assume responsibility for the plan. Participation also facilitated a common understanding of institutional purpose, budgetary constraints, and future projections.

2. *Budgeting processes sometimes improved.* Previously the president and the business manager had made all budget allocations. At some institutions, most notably Arkansas, budget making has become central to the planning process. Like planning, budget making can be highly participatory. At Arkansas, for example, over 75 percent of the persons interviewed indicated that the process was more decentralized; 90 percent felt that the process was equitable and that the persons involved possessed an adequate understanding of the issues; 100 percent indicated that there was an overall improvement in the total budgeting process. As results from interviews at a variety of other campuses also showed, there is more concern with budget

outcomes and costs when individuals have control in setting budgets and concomitant responsibility for spending.

3. *Institutional and program goals became clearer, more timely, and quantifiable.* Most respondents at our MBO institutions indicated that there had been significant improvement in the quality of goals submitted. The assessment of the previous year's goals and establishment of new goals became intimately linked to planning and evaluation. When program goals and objectives became the basis for evaluating performance, the specificity of the goals and objectives improved.

4. *Delegation of authority and decision making increased.* Most program directors indicated that the project had helped the president relinquish some of his control by delegating more authority and responsibility to the executive staff and program directors. Interviews and questionnaire data indicated a substantial increase in decentralization in most MBO institutions. Perceptions of faculty participation and support were high. Managerial activities were no longer confined to the top administrators.

5. *Legitimacy of decisions increased.* Extensive participation in planning, budgeting, evaluation, and decision making created a political environment that encouraged openness, trust, and compromise. As the participants shared more in the decision making, their willingness to abide by decisions increased. Participants almost always expressed a positive attitude toward the process. Most also indicated that, where consensus was lacking, there was still an understanding of the issue and an acceptance of the decision. In short, communication and morale increased on most campuses, and confidence in the leadership and administration of the colleges also increased.

6. *Managerial skills became more sophisticated.* Managerial participation and increased responsibility augmented the capabilities of second- and third-level managers. Administrative participation in a variety of seminars and workshops also increased managerial competence.

7. *An accurate, accessible data base was provided as an adjunct to decision making.* It soon became obvious that accurate and useful data are essential for planning. Interviews with top-level administrators indicated that financial and student data were the most useful. Due to the small size of the colleges,

there was little need for highly detailed faculty data and sophisticated enrollment data such as the Induced Course Load Matrix.

8. *Formalized plans proved to be effective tools to ensure that planning occurs.* The MBO projects provided the basic framework for planning on several campuses. The projects facilitated staff involvement in planning, which ultimately was the key to securing commitment to the plan and also stimulated faculty and staff consciousness about planning: the need to plan and the potential benefits that could be derived. The *process* itself, rather than the actual *plan* that emerged, became the critical element in the success of the effort. The Arkansas president summed it up in an interview: "Our MBO plan (SCAMP) is no better than a thousand other plans might have been; it only ensured that *planning actually happened.* It wouldn't have made much difference what plan was used, as long as the planning actually got done."

Problems and Lessons

Although the MBO projects seemed to be successful, we must realize that many of the positive claims were made by project directors and administrators who had vested interests in making the projects look good. The rosy claims must, then, be taken with a grain of salt. We do believe that most of the benefits listed above can come from a successful, mature MBO planning program. But we also learned a great deal about the problems and pitfalls that could—and *did*—plague an MBO project. From our studies we can outline some essential ingredients for success and list some potential problems that cause failure.

1. *Planning and budgeting are more successful when closely linked.* Budgeting has a tendency to become an adversary game when the final decision-making authority rests with one or two key administrators. And planning becomes a farce when it is not clearly tied to budgets and money. The separation of the two functions was unquestionably one of the biggest weaknesses in most MBO projects.

2. *If outside consultants are used, they must be selected with considerable care.* Outside consultants must be familiar with the unique characteristics of a small college's operations;

general knowledge of college and university administration is not sufficient. The typical management approach used by consultants in the corporate sector also presents significant drawbacks, usually presupposing a rigid hierarchy of authority and accountability. Well-selected consultants with management experience in a small-college environment can provide valuable expertise and assistance to staff members who probably have little management background.

3. *Presidential support and involvement in the process are essential.* Active presidential endorsement is essential to the management innovation's success. At both Arkansas and Furman, for example, presidential support extended beyond endorsement to total involvement as an ad hoc director and a member of the management team. At the conclusion of the projects, all respondents on campuses where those projects were successful indicated that the activities were supported by the chief administrator. Presidential support is not only essential for the initial phases of the project but will ultimately have impact on continuation once funding has ended.

4. *A realistic time frame to develop and implement a system is essential.* Even a small college is a complex organization. Development and implementation of an institution-wide MBO system impose considerable time demands on staff. Managers, for example, are required to have a broad perspective, be willing to compromise, and have some sophistication in leading others through the process. When a management innovation involves widespread organizational participation, there is potential for building throughout the college a team attitude that can improve resource utilization. But a hastily put-together program, poorly run, can have more negative than positive effects on the institution. At least three years are needed to undertake a project of any scope and complexity.

5. *The system must be simple to use.* Although the management information system projects were the most prone to information glut, the MBO programs also had tendencies in this direction. We were absolutely overwhelmed during one meeting with a project director who ran an MBO project. From his rows of bookcases, he pulled down dozens of "planning manuals." These manuals were supposed to be used by everybody in the

institution to plan the most minute details of work behavior. When we opened those manuals, we found hundreds of pages of forms, instructions, and workbooks. It was no great surprise to us to find, later, that most administrators, faculty members, and department heads in this institution complained bitterly about the "busywork" involved in the management by objectives program. In fact, the project finally came to a dull, grinding halt under the sheer weight of its form-happy nonsense. There was a form or a planning process for every conceivable step. Consequently, people soon found that they either had to fill out the forms or get their work done, and they chose to do the latter. Junk proliferation can overwhelm MBO projects just as it can MIS projects.

6. *The emphasis must be on planning, not on plans.* This point is most concisely summed up by Edward J. Green (1975, p. 2), president of Planning Dynamics: "Many people have been disappointed in planning because they expected too much and frequently the wrong things. Planning will not provide a perfect crystal ball, nor predict the future with accuracy, nor prevent mistakes, but a proper planning process will minimize the degree to which you are taken by surprise and help you revise objectives and programs when desirable. Administrators should judge planning not by whether they hit the original target, but by whether it helps optimize performance in a changing environment. During recent years planning has changed in nature, scope, and purpose. Managers are beginning to appreciate the significance of the military saying: 'Plans are sometimes useless, but the *planning process* is indispensable.' They used to think the sole purpose of planning was to produce a plan. Now they are starting to realize that a 'plan' is a valuable by-product (if it is flexible enough to respond to rapidly changing conditions); but the primary purpose of planning is to provide a better way of reaching and revising agreements. This requires a dynamic planning process."

Chapter Five

Applying Management by Objectives

In this chapter we will examine several case studies of institutions that combined their MIS project with a management by objectives effort. There were no cases where MBO was used alone; it was always combined with some type of MIS. However, we will focus on the MBO activities, since the information systems have been illustrated with other institutions. The three case studies are Furman University, Arkansas College, and Earlham College.

A Case Study of an MBO Project

Furman University is a Baptist, coeducational, liberal arts college in Greenville, South Carolina.* Founded in 1826, it cur-

*With minor changes the following material is quoted with permission from *Final Report: Furman University's Management Planning Model* by Philip C. Winstead, mimeographed, November 15, 1975, pp. 6ff.

rently has an undergraduate student body of approximately 2,100 and a faculty of 145. About twenty years ago, the university moved from a congested location in downtown Greenville to a spacious campus on the outskirts of town, and its curriculum was completely reorganized. A three-term calendar provides an academic program that permits independent study, foreign study opportunities, off-campus internships, and interdisciplinary courses. In addition to the undergraduate curriculum, Furman maintains small graduate programs in education, chemistry, and business administration.

Furman was not in serious financial or management difficulty when the new management-planning processes were introduced. Its administrators simply felt that many of their procedures could be improved.

The Furman Model

The model developed at Furman has three components: organizational development, information systems, and institutional research. We will focus here on organizational development, since the information systems and institutional research activities were discussed for other institutions in earlier chapters. There are several steps in Furman's organizational development activities.

Formulating Goals and Objectives. First of all, in 1970–71 Furman and four other institutions participated in an *institutional goals study* using the Delphi technique. This procedure helped Furman's administrators investigate what various constituents perceived the university's goals *actually were*, as well as what they *should be*. The study was made with a preliminary version of the Institutional Goals Inventory developed by the Educational Testing Service. The inventory contained a series of possible goal statements covering a broad range of college and university operations. In the summer and fall of 1972, the results of this study helped establish goals for the university as a whole and for each major organizational unit.

With goals as a foundation, each organizational unit established *measurable objectives* and adopted a management by objectives approach to administration. This approach was launched in June 1973 to correspond with the beginning of Furman's fiscal year. The starts were somewhat uneven in the various departments, depending on the personnel involved and their grasp of the techniques. To assist in this process, a workshop was held in October 1972 to help department heads analyze their goals, specify measurable objectives, and reach agreement with members of their staff in assigning responsibilities.

In actual practice, each functional unit is asked to do a "SWOTs" analysis each year; that is, each organizational unit examines its strengths, weaknesses, opportunities, and threats (SWOTs). The analyses from various units are then consolidated into a university-wide analysis. Thus, the SWOTs analysis provides a framework, with institutional goals and available resources, for establishing priorities among the proposed objectives. As a result, objectives can be authorized which maximize strengths, minimize weaknesses, capitalize on opportunities, and eliminate or minimize threats.

The system requires that objectives for each unit be set by members of that unit and reviewed by appropriate members of higher-level administration. At the higher echelons, the individual objectives are checked for consistency with other university objectives before they are authorized. Then an appropriate budget and responsibility for each objective are assigned to the appropriate person. The person is given wide latitude in achieving objectives but is required to provide frequent updates on progress. The employees and their supervisors hold quarterly review sessions. At the end of the fiscal year, the results are reviewed by employees and supervisors and compared with goals and objectives agreed on earlier. At this point, evaluation influences the reward system.

Securing Adequate Planning Data. Furman's administrators recognized at the outset the importance of effective planning. Specifically, planning should enable the institution and the participants to *accomplish optimum results*—the best results that can reasonably be expected in light of the circumstances—with less time, effort, and paperwork; *minimize surprise*—in the form of unexpected developments; *reach and revise agreement*; *coordinate different types of planning* (curriculum, financial, personnel, operations); *provide reliable information; achieve simplicity; maintain flexibility; and provide for effective participation.*

Since the quality of planning cannot consistently rise above the quality of the information on which it is based, accurate planning data must be readily available to all decision makers. Furman's procedure is to organize planning materials in a loose-leaf planning book. This approach provides for the controlled distribution and revision of important data. To minimize paperwork, outlines are used wherever practical, and written work is supplemented with improved individual communication, group discussions, and organized presentations.

The planning book is arranged in sections to answer a number of questions:

1. *Where are you?*
- Mission/Function. This section defines the scope and purpose of the program. No one can plan effectively for an activity until he or she understands what it is supposed to do.
- Environment/Competition. Pertinent data on important environmental and competitive factors are organized in this section. These include relevant information about general climate, economy, government, regulatory agencies, markets, attitudes, public relations, and competition.
- Capabilities/Opportunities. This section contains a critical objective analysis of an administrator's relative ability to conduct the particular program or activity in the face of competition.

2. *Where are you going?*
- Assumptions. Temporary estimates must be made of important probable developments.
- Goals/Objectives. Goals provide a general sense of direction or accomplishment. Objectives are estimates of desirable future results that the administrator believes can and will be achieved through his efforts within a given time period and for which he is willing and able to provide resources.

3. *How are you going?*
- Policies/Procedures. Policies are broad statements of general intent that tell what is permitted or expected. Procedures are more specific instructions that tell how things should be done.
- Strategies/Programs. Strategies and programs are the courses of action that enable an administrator to achieve his objectives.

4. *When are you going?*
- Priorities/Schedules. Priorities/schedules help determine and control who does what and what comes first.
5. *Who is going?*
- Organization/Delegation. This section deals with effective use of people.
6. *What will it cost?*
- Budgets/Resources. This section helps administrators get the right resources, in the right quality and quantity, at the right time and place, at the right cost. A properly developed budget should reflect approved programs of action with price tags.

A Successful Project?

Since 1971 Furman has been using the planning strategies outlined above. The chief activity during the final year of Exxon support was a formal evaluation of the program. An evaluation team visited the campus, examined the program, and prepared a written report on how well the objectives of the project had been met. The team consisted of Ralph Tyler, evaluation consultant, Science Research Associates and Harvard University; Peggy Heim, then director of evaluation, National Center for Higher Education Management Systems; and Dale McConkey, professor of management, University of Wisconsin.

Among the strengths listed were:

1. Management information system is relatively simple, can be maintained and updated at relatively low cost, and provides helpful reports.
2. Management information system has proved helpful in policy analysis, as well as in operational activities.
3. Availability of management data furthers openness.
4. Availability of data and openness contribute significantly to the institution's ability to cope with such situations as the unanticipated deficit that arose this year [1974–75].
5. Planning book is practical.
6. Structural organization for carrying the planning process functions well.

Among the weaknesses listed were:

1. Most planning has been on an annual basis or on a ten-year financial projection; to achieve desirable long-term growth, a better time frame would be three to five years.
2. Planning appears to be essentially an activity for administrators, department chairmen, and committee members; the faculty should be involved.
3. Follow-through is needed in academic areas.
4. No network or vehicle has been established by students to gather recommendations or to disseminate information to their fellow students.
5. Objectives are too broad and heavily oriented to activities rather than results.
6. Few academic departments have made notable progress in formulating their objectives; academic departments should be encouraged and helped to utilize management by objectives.
7. The annual budget is approved before all objectives and plans have been developed; this places the budget at the wrong end of the objective-setting process.

The visiting team concluded that "Furman has made excellent progress to date in implementing its management planning program." Furthermore, in a survey of ninety Furman administrators and department chairs, 76 percent of the respondents indicated that "the management planning program as it is currently in operation at Furman" should be continued in the immediate future. In short, most people felt that Furman had a successful project.

Transforming Management with an MBO System

Arkansas College is a four-year, independent liberal arts college. Located in the foothills of the Ozarks approximately 100 miles from the metropolitan centers of Memphis and Little Rock, Arkansas is the oldest private college in continuous operation in the state. Since its founding in 1872, the college has been affiliated with the Presbyterian church in the regional synod of the Red River. It is primarily an undergraduate institution with academic programs leading to a Bachelor of Arts degree. It also offers one- and two-year programs emphasizing occupational preparation in various fields.

Arkansas is a small college with a current enrollment of 450 students and a goal of increasing this number to 600 by 1980. The majority of students are full-time residents. The present recruiting program focuses on attracting "high-potential" students with less advantaged socioeconomic backgrounds from the immediate area. To assist this endeavor, generous financial aid has been made available to a substantial number of students. In addition to Presbyterian students, the student body represents a wide diversity of other religious affiliations.

Following a critical curricular review, the established offerings were supplemented and restructured to provide students with more options and better educational preparation for either graduate study, future professional training, or immediate entry into certain occupations. Traditional academic departments were eliminated and a core curriculum—plus four new programs in business management, health sciences, community services, and humanities—was developed. The core curriculum was designed as a basic interdisciplinary foundation for the other four programs; each of the four programs provided options for specialization.

Arkansas intends to remain a small college. Presently, the faculty numbers 44. The current student/faculty ratio is 10 to 1; even though the college goal is to accelerate enrollment growth, this ratio is not expected to exceed 20 to 1 in the future. As a result of recent recruiting efforts, 50 percent of the forty-four persons with faculty status have joined the staff during the last three years; academic competence and professional skill in teaching have also been improved.

Considerable attention is given to independent learning and individually designed instructional methods. Counseling services, also highly individualized, have become integral in each student's total academic program. Cooperative education in many fields is available to all students who wish to enroll. During the past three years, Arkansas has pursued several innovations, including a flexible academic calendar and experiential education. It is generally felt within the college community that the very smallness of the institution has facilitated greater experimentation and more student initiative and participation in the total learning process.

In 1974 the financial situation at Arkansas College was quite bleak. Like many small independent colleges, it was experiencing a decline in enrollments and an increase in operating costs. It also had some drawbacks in competing with surrounding institutions; among these were a considerably higher tuition, geographical isolation, and a physical plant that could not be called the ultimate in modernity. However, during the past five years the college has managed a remarkable fiscal recovery. The annual operating budget has grown almost threefold. An aggressive program for college development has been successful in securing over twenty foundation grants in addition to completing a well-subscribed capital campaign. Historically, the college has had a relatively small endowment, but since 1975 the fund has quadrupled. The college has also been able to garner a substantial amount of federal dollars through a vigorous college relations program with federal funding agencies.

In the early 1970s a tornado nearly destroyed the entire physical plant on the 100-acre campus, resulting in the construction and renovation of all buildings and athletic facilities. The college's physical structures have been modernized and now include well-equipped classrooms, laboratories, and a learning resource center.

The transformation at Arkansas has been quite extensive. The college has gone from an institution in a precarious financial posture to one whose future today is much more secure. Nevertheless, insufficient enrollment growth remains the most difficult problem facing the college. Presently, Arkansas is focusing on communicating its new academic image and developing more strategies that will raise college visibility and enhance its reputation to attract more students.

Early Planning Efforts

During the 1972–73 academic year, Arkansas engaged in an ambitious institutional evaluation and planning project involving all faculty, administrators, and many students. The study intended to examine all operational aspects of the college, including resources, services, faculty, and students. From this study massive data were gathered about the college.

To synthesize this information and the many reform proposals generated by task groups, the college established an Office of Institutional Evaluation and Planning. The office had as its main charge defining feasible means to operate the college efficiently, given the institutional goals, the current information base, and a limited resource structure. A steering committee—composed of the college president and administrators, together with faculty and student representatives—was established to review the proposed changes submitted by the task groups and the new plans proposed by the Institutional Evaluation and Planning Office. The process was arduous. Every attempt was made to base decisions on student needs and interests rather than on institutional traditions, faculty interests, or administrators' ambitions. Not all ideas or plans were accepted, but extensive changes did result. As one administrator noted, "The college emerged from the process significantly changed in many ways."

The college mission was reshaped. It included a commitment to serve students from more diverse backgrounds and to revise the curriculum so that the traditional liberal arts program would be complemented by a career preparation option. Ultimately, the curriculum was restructured into five programs that supplanted the previous divisions and constituent departments.

The administrative staff was reorganized into seven groups. Representatives from each group—the president's office, instruction, planning, athletics, guidance, advancement, and services—reported directly to the president. The groups were responsible for implementing policy decisions for the board and governing councils and making routine operational decisions.

As a direct result of the project, other important decisions were made: (1) to implement a college-wide program to improve teaching; (2) to introduce a new guidance program, stressing diagnosis and individualized counseling; (3) to establish a management by objectives process for institutional and individual goal setting; (4) to streamline the budget process; and (5) to restrict faculty size until the student body could grow to a point where the student/faculty ratio equals 20 to 1.

Once the formal evaluation and planning process was completed, the college initiated a plan to implement the new resolutions. Unfortunately, the process, albeit significant, was not as timely or complete as originally anticipated. Due to very limited resources, some important decisions were not implemented. Further, it soon became apparent to those closely involved that the college lacked the necessary management procedures and techniques to put the new plans into operation effectively.

As with many small colleges, Arkansas traditionally had functioned with a strong president who made many decisions for the institutions. Clearly, the president was accountable to the board of trustees for all phases of institutional performance, particularly fiscal responsibility. By assuming this leadership role, the president tended to retain control, thereby relieving other administrative officers of most decision-making responsibility. Therefore, when the administrative restructuring occurred at Arkansas, the appropriate decision-making authority commensurate with the administrative position was not always available. The concentration of authority remained with the president, and daily routine academic matters still received a significant amount of his attention.

Development of SCAMP

During this same period, Arkansas College learned about the Exxon Foundation's grant program. The director of institutional evaluation and planning developed a proposal to submit to the foundation. Arkansas College recognized that it needed to "increase its management efficiency through greater dispersement of decision making." As originally conceived, the project, Small College Academic Management Program (SCAMP), would address the issue of how to delegate decision making and accountability to second- and third-level college administrators. The president would act as a director-evaluator of his subordinates, rather than as an executor of all tasks; academic managers would assume responsibility for efficient direction and control of college activities. Distributing the management burden would allow the president more time to focus on his primary leadership functions. As described by the proposal writer: "The project would not decrease the responsibility of the institution's chief officer; it would change his method of directing the institution while upgrading the academic officers. It would permit these officers to become intimately involved in trying to achieve institutional goals, and free the president to exercise his primary leadership role, both internally and externally." It became imperative, first, to explore how a management accountability system could be established, based on the premise that the president would be willing to grant more authority and decision-making power to academic managers. Second, if academic managers were to assume responsibility for the operational aspects of college management, what skills and support services would they need to become effective? A transfer of the major management burden to subordinates would increase the delegation of authority. But it could also create many new difficulties if those receiving the authority were not equipped to use it.

Academic managers at Arkansas were viewed as resource persons whose skills needed sharpening to make maximum use of their expertise. Further, academic managers would require a more accurate, timely, and accessible data base to facilitate their decision making.

In March 1974, Arkansas College submitted its final proposal for SCAMP to the Exxon Foundation and, following notification of funding, began the implementation phase in January 1975.

Purpose and Expected Outcome of SCAMP. Briefly, the purpose of SCAMP was to (1) disperse decision-making power down to middle-management levels; (2) expedite the transition with appropriate management training, organizational structures, and support services; (3) develop a planning and budgeting cycle to improve decision making; and (4) improve the information base on which decisions were made. Ultimately, it was envisioned that the impact would be college wide. Specifically, the following outcomes were expected:

1. The college president would provide leadership but would not become involved in routine management activities. Decentralization of authority would occur.
2. Academic decision-making power would be given to second- and third-level managers.

3. Detailed and quantifiable goals would be set for all institutional segments.
4. Clear evaluation processes would be established throughout the college.
5. Basic data would be routinely gathered and quickly processed.
6. Timely and concise management reports would be available to provide information for decision making.
7. Management reports would be used routinely and effectively by academic managers.
8. Academic managers would become skilled in management and information use.

Planning and Budgeting Cycle. The heart of the Arkansas program is a planning and budgeting process that is repeated each year. It is important to review the steps in that procedure.

1. *Goal and objective setting for the institution and administrative components.* Each August the executive staff and the president participate in a retreat at which institutional goals are reviewed and evaluated. A similar process occurs for each administrative group. Goals and objectives are compared with actual performance. On the basis of this comparison, institutional goals are revised or modified, and new ones are set for each group. Each executive identifies the expectations she or he has for other administrative groups. All objectives are discussed, modified if necessary, and agreed on prior to the conclusion of the retreat. Preliminary overall budget guidelines for the upcoming fiscal year are also set at this time.

2. *Objective setting for program units.* During the next phase, the members of the executive staff and program directors meet jointly to discuss and review institutional goals. The group establishes priorities for the college and its various components and programs. Program directors, in turn, begin to work with their staffs to develop objectives and plan for the present and following years. Program directors also prepare cost estimates to accompany the plan and objectives. A deliberate effort is made not to use budgeted or audited expenditures from previous years as a decision-making basis.

3. *Budget review.* The next step in the process involves joint meetings of all executive administrators and program direc-

tors to review the objectives, plans, and budgets of all programs. The executive staff outline the overall financial position of the college—fixed costs, likely revenues, and general budget parameters. Meetings follow, during which considerable discussion and negotiation—"give and take"—occur. At the conclusion of this process, a completed budget emerges.

4. *Evaluation.* At the beginning of each calendar year, all program directors review the individual objectives and actual performances of all faculty and staff reporting to them. This review is followed by a conference with the executives, at which the performance evaluation is reviewed and salary, retention, promotion, and reassignment recommendations are agreed on. The same procedure is used by the president to evaluate the executives. Using performance evaluations and the corresponding recommendations, the president makes all final decisions on retention, promotion, and salary. These decisions are then incorporated into the final budget draft and submitted to the trustees.

5. *Planning.* Early in the summer following the performance evaluations, the executives and program directors evaluate their total operation to determine whether their goals and objectives have been met. At that time they identify future goals and establish priorities. This information is forwarded to the central administration as a basis for the retreat that will occur later in the summer. Thus, the whole cycle begins again.

During the last evaluation, planning, and budgeting cycle, the process included an additional dimension. The *Planning Guide*, the college's six-year long-range plan, was revised to reflect actual developments compared with projections. The modifications also included a revision of the institution's mission statement and overall goals, as well as updated projections for the next six years. This guide serves as a starting point for the planning, budgeting, and evaluation cycle.

Management Skills Training. It was critical to train the managers to use the planning cycle and the MIS network most effectively. Management training for executive administrators and program directors was accomplished by participation in college-sponsored seminars and workshops, by direct work with external management consultants, and by individual participation in management seminars, conferences, and professional training.

The SCAMP proposal, as originally conceived, relied heavily on outside consulting firms to provide training sessions, one-on-one consultations, and general assistance in operating the project. The college contracted the services of a private consulting firm but did not receive the type of assistance it requested or anticipated. Although the firm conducted several seminars, they were introductory in nature, and the appropriate follow-through did not materialize. Other than the preparation of an elaborate procedures manual, there was no substantive effort by the consultants to assist the college with the integration of SCAMP.

After nine months, the college decided to terminate the consulting contract and to contact several educational organizations to provide management expertise. From them the college obtained individual consultant services or appropriate referrals; these educational organizations also held training workshops and seminars.

The college communicated the information from these activities to other administrators through informal sessions. Despite the earlier unfortunate experience, administrators finally received the needed assistance and training which, combined with their intimate involvement with SCAMP, brought the positive results.

Administrative Reorganization. Administrative reorganization took place early in the project. The major administrative units in the college were now consolidated into six groups: the president's office, educational planning, admissions, advancement, development, and services. An executive administrator was appointed to direct each component. As "officers of the college," each executive reports directly to the president and, with the president, is a member of the executive staff. The executive staff depends on the dean of the college, as chief academic officer, to coordinate the annual planning, budgeting, and evaluation cycle.

Each administrative component of the college is organized into programs administered, in turn, by a director. Program directors and the executive staff make up the Educational Components Administrative Team (ECAT).

The reorganization significantly reduced the number of persons reporting directly to the president and dispersed administrative responsibilities and decision-making authority to second- and third-level administrators. As noted earlier, there are no departments or divisions at Arkansas. Faculty members are organized around programs, as are all nonteaching staff members.

The reorganization was a direct result of SCAMP. The management seminars, consultant advice, and college-wide discussion, together with the experience gained from the earlier evaluation and planning project, greatly facilitated successful completion of this segment.

Building a Management Information System. Arkansas was less enamored of the computer-based data-processing systems than were many other institutions that received RAMP grants. Arkansas viewed the MIS network as only a small piece of its project, while the other colleges focused almost exclusively on data gathering and processing. Nevertheless, Arkansas did recognize the need for a solid information base and for software to analyze it.

Prior to SCAMP, Arkansas relied minimally on computer services. Even such operations as registration, grade reporting, and accounting were performed manually. The effort to develop a limited management information system was difficult and slow. Two factors appeared responsible: first, the basic data-processing system was not complete and totally operative; second, the entire management system, although implemented, was not sufficiently intact to permit extensive development until the project was near completion.

When SCAMP began in January 1975, the college used a computer owned by a local bank. Midway through the project, the college purchased an IBM/3 computer and an additional complement of software. A small computer center with a manager for computer operations was established.

In selecting an appropriate data base, the college received excellent guidance from the Council for the Advancement of Small Colleges. Data bases used by other small colleges were also reviewed prior to the final selection of the composite data base. With the new computer hardware, two full-time staff members, and student assistant keypunch operators, the college devised a basic data-processing system to handle mass data. By the end of the project, accurate and complete systems were established for student records, enrollment analysis, financial aid, endowments, development funds, personnel information, and financial records.

When the project was terminated, two thirds of the proposed reports were available. Data generated by the system were used in the manual preparation of these reports. A schedule of revenues and expenditures, program budget status, financial aid usage, personnel positions, enrollments, and faculty and students were complete and available for administrative use. For those reports not yet completed, information was available, but it was either not in the computer or still in storage form.

This system, though far from perfected, is perhaps the single most impressive, tangible accomplishment of SCAMP. The college expects to use it in the future as an adjunct to decision making. It will make refinements where appropriate. Proposals to expand the system will be judiciously reviewed to prevent proliferation of a system inappropriate for a small college's operations.

Participatory Planning and Management by Objectives

Earlham—a private coeducational college with an enrollment of approximately 1,200 students—is primarily concerned with the education of undergraduate students in the liberal arts and sciences. It was founded in 1847 by the Religious Society of Friends on an 800-acre campus located in Richmond, Indiana, not far from Indianapolis. The academic program at Earlham leads to the Bachelor of Arts degree in twenty-one major fields within the sciences, humanities, social sciences, and physical education. The college also offers several interdepartmental programs in such contemporary fields as environmental studies, black studies, and human relations. Professional study in the ministry is available through the School of Religion. Numerous off-campus study programs for junior and senior students are conducted at educational centers in the United States and at foreign centers in Europe, the Middle East, Africa, and Asia.

The majority of students attending Earlham College are full-time resident students. Fifty-four percent are Protestant (of these, 20 percent are Quaker), 7 percent are Jewish, and 5 percent are Roman Catholic. The remaining students indicate no religious preference. Almost half of the entering freshmen plan to major in the social sciences. Medicine, law, education, research science, and social work rank high as professional career goals among Earlham students. Most students entering Earlham attended public secondary schools. Eighty-five percent of the entering freshmen were in the top quarter of their high school class. In recent years, approximately 50 percent of the students enrolled at Earlham have received financial assistance. Financial aid is provided by scholarships, work-study programs, grants, and loans, with the average award totaling approximately $1,800.

Earlham employs eighty-eight full-time teaching faculty members. Most classes beyond the introductory level are small, usually with ten to twenty students. Although it is a small college, Earlham has developed high-quality learning facilities, including a modern science center and a comprehensive academic library. The Earlham course of instruction emphasizes both a traditional curriculum and experiential learning. Students work closely with faculty members, and informal learning is encouraged. Central to Earlham's educational philosophy and continuing Quaker tradition is an emphasis on the experience of community and the Quaker consensus method for group decision making.

Like most other institutions, Earlham experienced little financial stress during the boom years of the 1960s. The planning process for the most part was superficial, and budget making was left almost entirely to the central administration. Although a faculty budget committee did exist, it met infrequently and had no significant influence on final budgetary decisions. In the mid 1960s the college established a long-range planning commission. However, its efforts were perceived by most faculty and staff members as ineffective, and administrative support was minimal. Eventually, the commission deteriorated into a powerless forum used primarily to exchange proposals for curricular reform.

By the early 1970s Earlham began to feel some of the same financial pressures that plagued other campuses. In 1972 the college began a three-year capital campaign drive as the initial phase of a ten-year fund-raising program. The documents prepared for the campaign generated serious skepticism, especially among faculty members, about the goals of long-range planning. Although the documents contained precise references to capital improvements and new buildings, they made only vague general references to curriculum, faculty development, and salaries. As one faculty member expressed it:

> Basically, the faculty at Earlham has a high trust of the administration. But, as the financial crisis got worse, we began to have uneasy feelings. And that slight discomfort became more painful when we saw the plans for the fund-raising campaign. It talked about all sorts of new buildings and new capital trust. Of course, it was a "capital" campaign specifically designed to raise money for the physical facilities. However, most of us on the faculty felt that it should have also had some emphasis on educational issues. And what was particularly nerve-racking was that at this very time the faculty began to be nervous about their salaries and about their job security. In short, we thought it was very short-sighted of the trustees and the administration not to include an emphasis on educational and faculty needs, as well as on the physical plant. And I think we all became a bit suspicious about the strong emphasis on "planning." More and more it seemed that planning meant planning for buildings, and, if anything, it was a threat to the faculty— planning might mean cutting back on faculty salaries or faculty positions.

Less than two years later, the $10 million campaign was substantially oversubscribed; during the same period, faculty size had been reduced and the average salary compensation had been increased annually. Some faculty fears, in retrospect, seem quite reasonable. By 1972 new building programs had used up a big chunk of the discretionary income. The subsequent cash squeeze required the college to borrow a half-million dollars to maintain its operations. In light of all these pressures, the college began to examine ways to improve the planning process.

Early Planning Efforts

In July 1972 a new provost and a new vice-president for business affairs took office, and the new provost took immediate responsibility for budgeting and planning. He designed a new plan of action to (1) establish a reliable *data base* for multiple-year budget comparisons, (2) develop a method for reporting and *monitoring budget performance*, (3) launch an annual *planning calendar* that would require earlier budget preparation and presentation, and (4) establish a strong broadly representative faculty-administrative growth and development fund for the next two years.

During this same period, Earlham began to experiment with more advanced budgeting procedures. With a number of other colleges, Earlham participated in a study of independent higher education in Indiana. Using the Resource Requirements Prediction Model, a computerized management information system (for an explanation of RRPM, see Chapter Two), Earlham studied the cost of instruction. With RRPM the college also built a model of the curriculum, which helped determine the real costs of various programs. By the early 1970s, Earlham was moving toward better cost analysis and more sophisticated budget projections. But those moves were really only scratching the surface of the college's financial problems.

The Long-Range Planning Project

In August 1974 a new president took office. Together with the provost, he continued to explore suitable methods that would coordinate budget making with long-range planning. Thus, Earlham College requested a grant from the Exxon Foundation to support a two-year program of planning development. The plan emphasized the traditional Quaker practice of wide participation as a means of reaching consensus on significant policy decisions. The proposal writers obviously felt that there would be significant improvement if more people in the college community understood the dilemma of steady-state financing and were more directly involved in the planning process. They anticipated that increased confidence in the benefits of the planning process itself would evolve from wider participation. Therefore, the Earlham project was a total college effort designed to meet the following objectives (condensed from *Planning at Earl-ham, 1975 and 1976*, a mimeographed document from the president's office):

1. *Improve the data base.* Inventory, analyze, and assess available data; identify further data needs and establish a planning research program.
2. *Clarify assumptions and goals.* Clarify college goals, priorities, assumptions, and forecasts.
3. *Improve staff planning skills.* Improve faculty and administrative planning skills through involvement in training workshops and the actual planning process.
4. *Coordinate and regularize the budget process.* Establish a regularly scheduled systematic procedure for planning and budgeting.
5. *Evaluate the "impact" of the planning effort.* Show the effect on the long-range plan itself and the total college.

Clearly, the major focus of the development program at Earlham was on the planning process. Expanded data gathering and analysis were mainly adjuncts to this process. This is a critical point. At many colleges we saw the data-analysis tail wagging the planning dog, but Earlham tried to put things in proper perspective. Planning was the activity; data gathering was only a tool to help that process.

The project was begun in 1974. Continuity in the planning project was sustained through the oversight of the Exxon Planning Group, which consisted of three senior officers, two support staff members, and the chairpersons of three major faculty committees. We will describe briefly each major objective of the Earlham project.

Improving the Information Base. The first task was to define the appropriate information needed for long-range planning. The planning group compiled an extensive inventory of reports on faculty staffing, enrollments, financial conditions, and curriculum. They found that definitions of such key elements as *students* and *faculty members* varied greatly from report to report; therefore, they tried to simplify and reconcile inconsistent quantitative data with similar labels. The extensive process of data gathering and analysis culminated in the publication of the *Earlham College Factbook*.

The first volume of the *Earlham College Factbook* contained approximately thirty data summaries on topics ranging from faculty teaching loads to financial aid costs. A year later the college released a second edition with expanded and updated materials. As data were consolidated and interpreted for various reports and summaries, it became increasingly apparent that much additional information would be needed to make planning decisions effectively. For example, it was almost impossible to determine the actual costs of most programs. There was a general feeling, for example, that physics and chemistry courses were expensive because of expensive equipment and small classes; but no one knew the actual differences in costs between these programs and, say, humanities courses.

Unfortunately, two significant transitions in the college administration occurred in the midst of the project. First, there was the installation of a new computer system, which was not functioning adequately for much of the project. This problem lessened the emphasis on establishing an extensive data base. Much of the information compiled for the *Earlham College Factbook*, for example, was hand-tabulated. Although the college had used the RRPM and had established an Induced Course Load Matrix (ICLM), the institution concluded that these models were too complex for a small college like Earlham. Therefore, in spite of a rather extensive plan for data gathering and processing, the effort turned out to be a considerably smaller portion of the total project than originally anticipated. Nevertheless, even with the more limited activities, the data base was strengthened considerably.

Clarifying Assumptions and Goals. Another major segment of the project was devoted to the clarification and articulation of college goals and objectives. The process was started when the president submitted to the board and the college community a tentative "mission statement" for discussion. This overall mission was later translated into specific goals and the goals, in turn, into operational objectives. These, too, were presented to the campus community. Consistent with its Quaker practice, Earlham sought college-wide participation. In a series of discussions, faculty members and administrators examined the proposed goals and objectives. About 75 percent of all faculty members and administrators attended these meetings. Suggestions were gathered, and a refined set of goals and objectives was subsequently reported to the faculty and staff members.

Later, the planning group conducted a three-day workshop to clarify college goals further. That session studied the relationship of the goals to the educational program, the Quaker identity of the college, the demographic patterns, and the fiscal structure. Twenty-five faculty members, administrators, and trustees participated. The documents produced at the conclusion of the workshop outlined twelve major goals for the college, together with supporting operational objectives. These statements are examples of the goals:

1. To develop our common life by extending our understanding of Quaker business procedures based on them.
2. To engage students in depth in a field of concentration.
3. To concentrate on the achievement of individual progress, independence, and responsibility by our students.
4. To foster and support educational innovations which strengthen the liberal arts program.
5. To increase faculty effectiveness, productivity, and satisfaction.
6. To maintain an enrollment of 1,000 full-time-equivalent students on campus.
7. To employ budget procedures that will cope with a shortfall of students or income without serious jeopardy to our educational goals.

While these goal-setting activities were occurring, members of the college community had to test the goals against reality; they had to clarify their real-world assumptions about finances, enrollments, and the competition of other colleges. Specifically, one major question faced the planners at Earlham: "How, and to what extent, can aggregate demographic data and economic trends be used as realistic contexts for small-college planning?" Although the college recognized that planning would have to operate within a framework of assumptions, the selection of *relevant* assumptions remained a delicate task for the administration. For example:

1. The national enrollment projections look slightly down, but are the local conditions such that Earlham will actually face a decrease in enrollment?
2. The inflation rate for the nation has been quite high and may be high again in the future, but how can Earlham predict the inflation rates? How can it deal wisely with endowments without an accurate prediction?
3. Can Earlham maintain its distinctive Quaker atmosphere and still attract enough students to sustain the budget? The state of Indiana is changing its policy about public colleges. How will this change affect Earlham's competitive position within the educational market?

In all these areas—and many more—the planners had to anticipate the future and make a series of assumptions on which the planning could be based. And they did spell out their critical underlying future projections. We need not go into detail on those projections, but the planning process involved not only quasi-scientific analyses of data but also some educated guesses about the future of the economy, the enrollment pool for Earlham, and the competition from other colleges.

Near the conclusion of the project's second year, a refined statement of goals and objectives, together with select underlying assumptions, was presented to the board and faculty. The outcome of these two major undertakings was to link general college goals and concrete objectives with realistic assumptions, feasible plans, and available resources. For the many faculty and staff participants, it proved an instructive and sobering experience. The plan involved (1) a "no-growth" policy for enrollment; (2) continued emphasis on residential student housing; (3) a commitment to keep salaries up with at least cost-of-living increases; (4) a leveling off, and perhaps a reduction, in the size of the faculty; and (5) less emphasis on new buildings and construction.

Improving Staff Planning Skills. To support the planning efforts, the college held three training workshops for faculty members and administrators. Outside consultants were retained to assist in the design and leadership of the training sessions. In one session the consultants demonstrated how computer techniques could help in the planning process. Using the Earlham data base, they devised a series of simulation exercises, in which participants tried to determine how various factors—such as changes in the recruitment pool, tuition, staffing, enrollments, and inflation—could affect the budget. The participants were introduced to simplified budgeting techniques, and they participated in decision-making simulations that required assessments of the long-range implications of various decisions. In effect, using an exercise on the computer, they saw how all the elements in a complex decision are interwoven.

The workshops proved enlightening. For many, it was the first exposure to even the simplest computer-assisted models that could facilitate planning. The simulations demonstrated vividly how seemingly small, unconnected decisions could have an enormous impact on the future educational and fiscal well-being of the college and its various departments.

Coordinating and Regularizing the Budget Process. Several modifications in budgetary processes were necessary if budget-making practices were to be coupled more effectively to long-range planning. As a beginning step, all department heads of both academic and support services were asked to prepare statements of goals and objectives, along with a description of their programs and their personnel plans. On completion of these two tasks, they were also asked to identify corresponding resource requirements: What would it cost to achieve the goals? These program plans and their corresponding budget requests were compiled into two separate volumes: Volume 1 included plans for the next academic year; Volume 2 outlined long-range plans for two to five years. The two volumes were available to all department heads and their staff for review. The goal was to identify overlaps and potential linkages and also to foster understanding about other college segments, plans, goals, and resource needs. An unanticipated side effect was that, while *understanding* increased, *competition* also developed between departments for the limited resources.

In an attempt to tie down these diverse planning efforts to a coordinated institutional plan, the college established a five-year budget-planning cycle. The first phase called for yearly departmental meetings with all personnel. Discussions focused on both short- and long-range plans and resource needs. The department chairperson used the information from these meetings to prepare a plan, which was then submitted to the responsible administrator (a vice-president) for initial study and feedback. The vice-presidents were responsible for coordinating and revising the unit plans in their areas into "sector" plans, which were then available to the president and the administrative council for review and adaptation for a College Plan, as environmental constraints and institutional policies required. These plans all included fiscal components relevant to budget building.

Following presidential review, the College Plan was forwarded to the college budget committee, where it was discussed with department heads, adjusted if necessary, and returned to the president for approval. The short-range plans were submitted to the board of trustees for approval, while the long-range plans were presented to the board for discussion.

As a last measure to improve the budget-planning process, two formal provisions for fiscal contingencies were introduced. Given the probability of enrollment fluctuations and changes in other financial conditions, a contingency pool was established within the regular budget. A skeleton contingency budget, which prepared for a cut if necessary, was built parallel to the regular budget. Both the actual and contingency budgets were projected on alternative assumptions of enrollment size and other fiscal variables for the five-year period corresponding to the college plan. The contingency concept was recognized as extremely useful, and its incorporation into the total college budget was well received.

Successful Features of the Project

Planning, budget making, and decision making became more systematic, and much broader, rather than essentially localized. All departments and units of the college were included. The reevaluation of college mission, goals, and objectives involved the entire teaching and administrative staff. The five-year planning and budgeting cycle included all college units; faculty and administrative representatives participated in training workshops and planning simulations. Many data sources were inventoried and data needs reassessed. In short, few areas of the college were left unaffected.

In an attempt to assess the impact of the Exxon project on planning, the college and external evaluators conducted several studies. One overall statistic is notable: Of the administrators who responded to our survey, 67 percent said that the college would have been justified in starting the project even without outside funding; 17 percent said "maybe"; and 16 percent said "no."

Earlham faculty and staff members became more fiscally sophisticated and planning oriented during the project. The following conclusions were derived from our interviews and from questionnaire data.

1. *There was widespread support and acceptance of the planning process itself.* The extensive involvement of faculty members with the administrative staff in arriving at a consensus about the college mission, future goals for the educational program, and resource needs was particularly effective in securing commitment for a structured long-range plan. As a consequence, 83 percent of the respondents in our survey said that the "planning" process has changed for the better.

2. *The realities and implications of future enrollments and economic trends on the total educational program are now better understood.* The ability of the administrative and teaching staff to perceive the relationship between educational goals, program operations, and fiscal decisions has been markedly enhanced by the training workshops. Rather than simply constructing "wish lists," department chairmen and deans are much more sensitive to the budgetary realities that accompany their educational goals. A comment from one department chairman vividly illustrates this change in attitudes:

> The new planning procedures have definitely helped me a lot. That is especially true since I'm now forced to look at the budgetary implications of my plans. To be honest, in the past, when the budget and the plans were separate activities, I usually constructed a wish list. I assumed Santa Claus

was coming to town and I could ask for any damn thing I wanted. Now I realize that Santa Claus was a figment of my imagination, and I'm going to have to pay for anything on my wish list. With that reality testing, my plans have come down off the clouds and have become firmly planted on the hard ground of common sense. It is interesting to watch the attitudes of the faculty in my department change too. Now that they realize they have more responsibility for allocating the budgets, I feel that they are much more responsible about the decisions they make. That is not to say they weren't responsible before, but their feet are held to the fire more now. They have to connect their grand plans with a small pot of money.

3. *There is a greater recognition of institution-wide problems.* Many people whom we interviewed commented on their increased sensitivity to total institutional problems. In turn, this wider institutional perspective enabled them to plan better within their respective units, taking into account the larger context of the entire college.

4. *Interdependency among departments was highlighted.* Many faculty and staff members also expressed a greater understanding of the operational and fiscal interdependency that existed among the various college units. Most people felt that this would, in the future, facilitate more extensive communication between college subunits about critical planning and budgetary issues. As the different college units realized that their activities and decisions could profoundly affect the activities of other segments of the college, the tendency to consult with groups that might be affected was enhanced.

5. *The legitimacy and political acceptability of decisions were increased.* Wide participation in the college and departmental planning sessions and workshops assisted in creating a political environment that encouraged support of the new planning and budget-making strategies. Decision-making procedures were sufficiently public and involved enough people to increase the legitimacy of those decisions. Many administrators and faculty members commented that their involvement in planning and

budgetary decision making had been more extensive during the past two years than in any of their previous years at the college. In our survey, 84 percent of the Earlham administrators felt that the faculty supported the project.

6. *Faculty opinions about planning and governance improved.* Surveys of faculty and staff members seemed to show that their opinions of "democratic governance" and "quality of planning" had improved. The college administered questionnaires from the Institutional Functioning Inventory, developed by the Educational Testing Service, to the faculty. Results were analyzed for changes over the five-year period from 1971 to the conclusion of the project. The results indicated that faculty members perceived a significant increase in the effectiveness of self-study and planning at the college, moving from a 32 percent "favorable" response in 1971 to a 66 percent response at the conclusion of the project. In addition, the average faculty rating on democratic governance moved up ten percentage points to the 94th percentile during the project.

Data gathered by the research team at the conclusion of the project support these findings. Our survey indicated that faculty participation in the setting and implementation of objectives and in budget making had significantly increased since the inception of the project. Faculty understanding of the key issues in these processes had also increased. However, 67 percent of the administrators in our survey suggested that even *more* faculty training would have been helpful.

Several administrative areas also showed considerable change as a result of the Exxon project, especially financial aid, the budget committee, and middle management.

1. *Financial aid activities, a crucial and complex element in college operation, were revised following a cash-flow analysis.* Status reporting and data analysis have become more sophisticated and frequent. The college undertook a policy of more limited scholarship aid, with a greater preference for loans.

2. *The budget committee shifted its emphasis from detailed work on budgetary items to broader areas of analysis.* It began a series of regular discussions on budgetary problems with faculty members and administrators. It also conducted additional sessions for students about financial aid. When financial prob-

lems were imminent, the committee set reduction goals to be met in broad organizational areas, rather than designating specific areas for budget reductions. This approach helped return decision making to the administrators of the various college units. The budget committee also established a system for periodic reviews of current budgets and a procedure for submitting short- and long-range budget estimates and projections. In sum, instead of reviewing each line item, the committee managed to focus on larger issues and general procedures.

The improvements in the budgeting process are vividly shown in our survey of administrators, where we found strong expressions of support. Sixty-seven percent felt that the process was more equitable; 100 percent felt that the involved parties understood the issues better; 50 percent felt that the procedures were more systematic; 83 percent felt that there was more faculty participation; 60 percent felt that the process led to more effective use of resources. And, to top it off, 83 percent of the administrators felt that there had been an overall improvement in the budget process.

3. *Middle-level administrators developed plans that were more detailed and precise.* Planning became systematized, with attention given to the long-range future as well as to the next year. Administrators began working more closely together on planning and budget making. The availability of more comprehensive data contributed substantially to decisions on programs and staffing.

4. *The position of planning officer was accepted and established in the college budget.* Support for this new position was widespread. Most staff members felt it would be essential to have this person report directly to the president to maintain the integrity of the position. The planning officer helped institutionalize the planning process. Instead of an ad hoc process conducted once a year with no continuity, the process was placed on a firm ongoing basis.

Shortcomings of the Project

Faculty members and administrators had two major criticisms of the planning project.

First, there was a weak link between planning and budget making. A few faculty members felt that many planning sessions were merely exercises and that final decisions about programs and resources were still made by the central administration in the absence of discussion. Although there was a series of college-wide planning sessions and workshops, it was generally agreed that they provided only an "informal context" in which broad decisions were made. As one unhappy department head put it, "The process as presently structured results in a truncated process of decision making where plans and budgets are submitted by college units and departments but no formalized procedure has been established for review, feedback, discussion, or negotiation." Middle-management administrators, department heads, and their respective faculties sometimes claimed that they lacked a formal communication channel through which their plans and resource needs could be articulated and justified.

Interviews indicated that the central administration recognized the weak link between the planning and budgeting process. The top administrators said that, in future planning cycles, departmental plans would be tied more closely to the total college plan and the planning and budgeting cycle. A few people, however, were openly skeptical of the administration's willingness to make such changes.

The other area most frequently cited as less than adequate was the data system. There was an ambivalence about this issue. In our *survey* the vast majority of administrators (over 80 percent on most questions) felt that student and faculty data had improved. But in our *interviews* many people expressed a need for a more useful and comprehensive data base. The workshops had convinced potential users of the benefits of a data network as a tool for decision making. Unfortunately, the computer system was not operative for much of the project. The program software was also a problem. Earlham hired several consultants to advise on the initiation of the data system. In the early phases of the project, they considered the RRPM system. However, as noted earlier, the college decided that the RRPM was too complex for its needs. The difficulty in using some of the standard RRPM software programs was noted at several other colleges during our research. Earlham turned to a simpler data-analysis procedure, feeling that a simpler system would be more flexible and more adaptive to its needs. No sooner had the new system been installed, however, than difficulties with the computer began. As a result, the data-analysis process was not as central to the Exxon project as originally envisioned. At the time of our final interviews at Earlham, the new computer was running well, and the new software program was being adapted to meet the needs of the college. The Earlham administration fully expected that data analysis would be more successful in the future.

Summary

Declining resources provided an incentive for Earlham College to develop new processes for planning, budgeting, and decision making. The college implemented a two-year broad-based institutional planning program funded by the Exxon Foundation. The goal was to preserve the educational integrity of the college while maximizing its flexibility in using staff, funds, and space.

Strong administrative leadership from the provost and the president gave critical impetus to starting the program. The involvement of faculty members with administrators from all segments of the college remained, perhaps, the most critical prerequisite for both the initial success and the continuation of the project. From the very beginning, the college sought wide participation. A series of faculty-administrator workshops was successful in raising the general level of consciousness about the problems of the institution and its future. The strategy was most effective in securing, first, recognition of the need to plan and, second, a commitment to new methods for planning. These training sessions encouraged efficient and open communication. The groups included people from many segments of the college. Decision-making procedures were sufficiently participative to minimize conflict. Broadly based institutional involvement afforded little opportunity for any department or group to adopt a "wait-and-see" attitude. This wide participation was fostered by the college's deep roots in the Quaker tradition of consensus and shared decision making.

Clearly, during the two-year project there was more emphasis on the *process* of planning itself than on the plans. Involvement was a key to securing commitment to the process. Considerable review and discussion time was spent in preparing a well-defined college mission statement and accompanying goals. Despite the drawback of the time required, the increased participation supports the notion that decisions seem more legitimate to participants when they have taken part. Thus, participation reduces the likelihood of subsequent opposition.

Not everything was consensus, however, for a number of people complained that the process of final budget allocation remained closed to participation except for the central administration. Many people felt that there had been a genuine attempt to decentralize authority in the planning process but that the need for close financial controls had maintained the inevitable tendency toward centralization. This was the one aspect of the entire project most frequently criticized.

Claims for the program should not be overplayed. By and large, the campus community felt that the project was a success. However, some felt that the potential outcomes had been overstated, making the real project suffer by comparison. At the same time, most staff felt that the project cost had not been excessive and that the benefits had easily justified the expenditure.

The two-year project had intrinsic value for many participants. Increased depth of understanding of institutional problems and a willingness to continue institutional planning efforts are most notable. For the college, the value of the project will be proved or disproved in future operations. At Earlham, there is substantial agreement that broad-based institutional planning is necessary for college survival, that both faculty and administrative participation is necessary, and that meaningful planning requires an adequate data base. Planning decisions were derived more from concern and understanding, shared goals, and political realities than from a concrete data analysis. It is reasonable to expect that the Earlham planning capabilities will be refined and extended, utilizing past experiences, human expertise, professional judgment, and modern computer technology.

Chapter Six

Measuring the Financial Impact of Management Systems

"It is only by careful economies, in addition to new sources of income, that the liberal arts college will be able to survive the financial pressures of the next few years" (Millett, 1952). These words, a quarter of a century old, seem equally pertinent today. In the first part of this decade, Cheit (1973) found that the average increase in operating expenditures for colleges and universities was 8.1 percent. The corresponding increase in operating revenues per full-time-equivalent (FTE) student was 4.8 percent. The resulting gap between expenditures and revenues was labeled the "cost-income squeeze" of this "new depression" in higher education (Cheit, 1971). Increased costs, not lower revenues, were the primary difficulty. Higher costs were due largely to four factors: inflation, labor-intensive educational technology, increased responsibilities, and enrollment growth.

Inflation hurts colleges just as it does other institutions. The cost of goods and services is spiraling, as everyone knows.

These goods and services include laboratory materials, supplies and equipment, and academic and nonacademic salaries. Because educational institutions use specialized resources, the cost of these goods and services increases at a faster rate than the consumer price index. Thus, general inflationary pressures increase institutional expenditures, and this trend is reinforced by the extra cost increases in the specialized resources that colleges need. Moreover, unlike many industries, higher education cannot seek relief from inflation through technological improvement. Educational technology yields few demonstrable gains in productivity. Since colleges are unable to offset higher labor costs by increases in productivity, the cost per student increases relative to the rest of the economy.

Another factor contributing to an acceleration of institutional expenditures is the increased responsibility assumed by private universities and liberal arts colleges. In the case of private universities, there has been increased coverage of new, specialized fields in medicine, computer science, space technology, agriculture, and so on. The use of sophisticated new equipment and procedures has added to pressure for increased expenditures (Bowen, 1969). Graduate study has also received more emphasis. With the increase in the proportion of graduate students have come lower faculty work loads in graduate courses, smaller classes, and more senior faculty teaching in graduate programs. In short, the educational task is more complex than ever, and the costs reflect that complexity.

Private universities and liberal arts colleges are faced with increasing costs in the nonacademic areas as well. Increased staffing of student service and development offices has added substantial costs. The major building campaigns of the golden years of the 1960s have left the institutions with huge building maintenance costs and large debt-service bills. Finally, student aid has been one of the fastest-growing costs (Jenny and Wynn, 1970).

Costs have been increased by another factor: larger enrollments. Conventional wisdom says that there is often an economic advantage in enrollment growths, because they are "economies of scale" that generally reduce operating expenditures per student. However, many administrators learned to their dismay that those economies of scale worked only when the larger enrollments could be handled within existing space and personnel limitations. Without this unused capacity, increasing the number of students would add substantial institutional costs. In fact, without careful planning, additional students can push the institution to a new cost threshold and cause it to lose all advantages of scale.

In the face of these spiraling costs, institutions frantically searched for new revenues and for better management techniques to reduce costs. One primary objective of the Exxon Education Foundation's Resource Allocation Management Program (RAMP) was to help institutions control their costs and balance their budgets. The general assumption, shared by both the foundation and the institutions, was that strong management information systems would produce more rational decision making and thus help reduce expenditures. Since finances were such important elements in the original objectives, we are devoting two chapters to financial issues. Here we will examine the *specific* impacts of the RAMP projects on instructional costs. In Chapter Nine we will move to a more general examination of institutional cost control.

Measuring Instructional Costs

We had to establish standardized expense measures that would be comparable across all the institutions. We could not determine the impact of RAMP without first getting the straight picture about expenses. This task was much more difficult than it appeared on the surface. How do we establish comparable cost measures across a range of institutions with differing purposes, complex mixtures of graduate and undergraduate programs, complicated patterns of residence and commuter students, and a thousand other differences to complicate the cost analysis? Here is how we did it:

First, we concentrated on "departmental direct costs." Rather than measuring the thousands of different cost items, we decided to focus on three expenses: (1) faculty salaries, (2) the salaries of nonacademic departmental personnel, and (3) departmental supplies and equipment. In other words, we focused on the educational program, eliminating such items as dormitory costs, sports activities, physical plant, and other items that might not be comparable from one institution to another.

Second, we concentrated on several academic departments. The distribution of courses in an academic program might pose a serious threat to the comparability of instructional costs between institutions. For instance, a college with 75 percent of its courses in the humanities will have a different instructional cost structure than one that devotes 75 percent of its academic program to physical sciences. Consequently, to ensure comparability between institutions, we collected cost data from only a few academic departments: biology, English, mathematics, philosophy, political science, and psychology. These departments were selected for two reasons. First, they are common to all institutions. Second, they are representative of the various major divisions in a typical liberal arts program: humanities, natural sciences, and social sciences. We do not necessarily assume that inferences from these departments are generalizable to the institution's total instructional costs, but at least they give *some* information comparable from one institution to the next.

Third, total direct costs were sometimes deflated by the inflation rate. This adjustment allowed us to study trends in instructional costs of both "current" (not deflated) and "constant" 1967 (deflated) dollars. Government statistics often use 1967 dollars as the baseline; so we did likewise. The use of "constant" dollars did show one startling fact. In constant 1967 deflated dollars, the money spent on instruction—even in the face of much rhetoric about runaway costs—has actually *declined*. More on this later.

Fourth, we adjusted for graduate student enrollment. Even though most of the RAMP institutions were private liberal arts colleges, some private universities with graduate programs were included. In addition, some liberal arts colleges have small graduate programs, usually in education and business administration. Thus, some adjustments for the extra costs of graduate education were necessary. Most graduate programs at the RAMP institutions were in the less expensive disciplines of education and business administration, so we assumed that the cost per graduate student was roughly three times greater than the cost per undergraduate student. When we studied costs, then, the number of graduate students was tripled and added to the number of undergraduate students.

Fifth, to control the size, we divided the total departmental costs by the number of FTE students enrolled in each department. One FTE undergraduate student was defined as thirty semester credit hours per year; one FTE graduate student equaled twenty-four semester credit hours per year.

Sixth, we converted any quarter credit hours to semester credit hours by multiplying them by .67.

To summarize, then, we wanted to construct an expenditure measure that would be comparable across many different institutions. Consequently, we focused on direct departmental expenditures in departments that were common to all the institutions. Then we made a series of adjustments for the size of the department, the number of graduate students, and quarter versus semester hours. All the figures in charts throughout this chapter have been adjusted in this manner. Furthermore, we sometimes adjusted for the inflation rate so that we could study costs in "constant" dollars.

Overview of Findings

The results of our specific analysis can be summarized in the following statements:

1. There was an overall *reduction* in instructional costs for all types of institutions when we discounted for inflation.
2. Colleges with successful management information systems showed a narrowing of costs per student between departments; the cost variation between departments was reduced.
3. Colleges that successfully implemented advanced management information systems made larger reductions in their per student instructional costs.
4. Colleges that implemented MIS programs early had more cost reductions than those that implemented late.
5. Cost reductions were accomplished primarily through increases in the student/faculty ratio, due to larger student

enrollments, and by faculty salary increases lower than the inflation rate.

6. Interviews in institutions with cost reductions suggested that the increase in student/faculty ratios was partly due to the management information systems. The systems were having the intended impact on decision making.

It is important to make one point clear: Our conclusions about the financial effects of the projects are highly tentative, because there were many problems in analyzing the cost impact. First, it was necessary to have some "time lag" for the projects to have impact. They did not come in one day and have impact the next; we guessed that it would take at least three or four years. Since many projects simply did not have the appropriate time lag, it was difficult to tell what impact they were having. Second, many institutions were unable to give us reliable data for the entire time period. Third, we decided to focus almost exclusively on the management information systems, rather than on the management by objectives programs, because the MBO projects were not specifically oriented toward cost reductions. Finally, many other things were affecting the institutions besides the RAMP projects. *All* higher education institutions were grappling with cost problems during this period. Many things were happening: enrollment changes, federal aid changes, shifts in state support, and runaway inflation.

Analysis of Findings

With the problems of analysis and with these external changes, it behooves us to be modest in our conclusions. We must be cautious in attributing changes in expenditures and financial status to the RAMP projects. We think there is a *hint* that the MIS projects helped reduce expenditures, but that is about all we can say, because the situation is much too complex to make definitive statements. This chapter will examine some trends, some hints, some vague patterns. We believe that, taken together, these hints and patterns suggest that the MIS projects were partially successful in reducing costs. However, we make no bold claims where the data cannot justify them. Let us examine our findings one by one.

Reduction in Value of Resources for Instructional Activities

Departmental expenditures per student in *current* dollars increased at an average annual rate of 4 percent between 1972 and 1975. However, this growth in expenditures was substantially *less* than the growth in the consumer price index, thus leading to a decline in expenditures per student expressed in *constant* (deflated) dollars. Departmental costs for each type of Exxon project are shown in Table 6 in "constant" 1967 dollars.

The decline in the real value of instructional costs has been suggested in previous studies. Minter and Bowen (1977) noted that there has been relative stability in the expenditures for private institutions. However, they realized that analyzing instructional and noninstructional expenditures together—which they did—may mask important trends. Specifically, they suggested that "because of rising costs in the nonsalary areas—for example, energy—the institutions have not been able to give full cost-of-living salary increases to faculty and staff." This explains precisely what we have found in the Exxon institutions, as we will show later in this chapter.

Equalized Expenditures Among Departments

As any university administrator knows, there is wide variation in the costs of academic programs. Undergraduate engineering programs, for example, often cost three or four times more than graduate programs in many social science departments. Chemistry and physics departments have unusually high expenditures for supplies and laboratories. Agricultural programs have substantial investments in land and equipment. By contrast, most humanities and social science programs are relatively inexpensive.

Management information systems can highlight, expose, and publicize the differences in cost among departments. In many institutions the information from the data bank was startling to department chairpersons—especially those in the low-cost departments who felt cheated because others were living on

Table 6. Average Departmental Expenditures per FTE Student (Constant 1967 Dollars)[a] (23 Institutions with Exxon Grants at Any Point During 4 Years)

Category of College	1972–73	1973–74	1974–75	1975–76	Average Annual Growth Rate, in Percentages	Average Growth for 4 Years, in Percentages
Least Successful (N = 35 depts.)						
Mean ($\bar{X}$)	951	1,145	1,123	1,155	5	21
Standard Deviation	(626)	(522)	(501)	(551)		
Too Early to Tell[b] (N = 34 depts.)						
Mean ($\bar{X}$)	708	585	589	570	–5	–19
Standard Deviation	(324)	(203)	(155)	(196)		
Successful Data-Bank MIS (N = 21 depts.)						
Mean ($\bar{X}$)	1,145	1,076	1,167	1,093	–1	–5
Standard Deviation	(564)	(497)	(477)	(453)		
Successful Advanced MIS (N = 30 depts.)						
Mean ($\bar{X}$)	1,408	1,320	1,239	1,155	–5	–18
Standard Deviation	(896)	(743)	(702)	(533)		
Successful MBO (with MIS) (N = 21 depts.)						
Mean ($\bar{X}$)	777	712	672	678	–3	–13
Standard Deviation	(346)	(275)	(216)	(231)		
All Departments (N = 141)						
Average ($\bar{X}$)	994	967	926	953	–1	–4
Standard Deviation	(628)	(605)	(667)	(693)		

[a]Deflated by the consumer price index in which the reference year is 1967.

[b]The decrease in this category is due to huge decreases in *one* institution. Without it the average annual rate would be 4 percent, and the total rate from 1972 to 1975 would be 16 percent.

a much grander scale. One English department chairman fumed: "I've always known we were the cheapest department and that we were getting the short end of the stick. But I didn't know *how badly* we were getting the shaft. Shortly after the first figures came out, we had a departmental meeting. We plotted how we could get a bigger share of the pie. I don't think we've really been successful. But we put the heat on the dean to draw the Big Spenders back in line!" On the other side of the fence, the Big Spenders were really feeling the pinch: "I'm the chemistry department chairman. This damn new system of passing all the cost figures around to the department chairmen has certainly put the heat on us. We have always been expensive, but now we feel like we're standing in the limelight, and everyone is standing around clucking their tongues about how extravagantly we run our department. At the last department heads meeting, we discussed budget matters even though it wasn't on the agenda. And the bottom line was simple: The department chairmen in the less expensive departments are screaming bloody murder about getting our costs down. And it was obvious that the dean was tickled pink, chuckling under his breath to see the other department chairmen doing his dirty work for him!"

From testimony such as this and from interviews with deans and vice-presidents, we realized that a major impact of the MIS networks was to publicize departmental differences and to generate pressure for narrowing these differences. The figures were now "in the limelight," and this public exposure promoted a great deal of discussion about "fair play" and "extravagance." Many people echoed the chemistry chairman's comment that the social pressure from less expensive departments was even more effective in reducing cost differences than administrative pressure.

Did the empirical data show a narrowing of the expenditure gap? They most assuredly did. Tables 6, 7, and 8 have information about average departmental expenses. The mean ($\overline{X}$) shows the amount that the typical department spent; the standard deviation shows the *variation* around that mean. In other words, the mean shows what the "typical" departments were doing, while the standard deviation shows how much scatter there was around the typical situation. The larger the standard deviation, the larger the spread around the mean and the greater the variation among departments.

The facts are clear in all three tables. Institutions that had successful management information systems *reduced* the variation among departments from 1972 through 1975. By contrast, those that did not successfully implement management information systems generally had *increases* in variation. This reduction in variation among departments was particularly pronounced in the institutions with advanced MIS. It appears that the public exposure of careful information, generated by MIS, was one factor in reducing the variation among departments. The testimony of deans and department chairpersons is solidly supported by our data on costs.

Would the variations among departments have been reduced without MIS? Our guess is that they would have. Our interviews indicated that the administrations were determined to reduce those variations regardless of whether they had an MIS. However, the use of an MIS supported that determination, provided the objective facts and figures, and made the variations public. The determined resolve of administrators was supported by the right data available at the right time. We are not arguing that MIS *caused* the reduction in variation among departments, but we are arguing that these *helped* push a trend that probably would have happened anyway.

We should ask ourselves why the trend toward reducing variations is not as clear in the "least successful" institutions. There are probably two reasons. First, systematic data were not as public in those institutions. The absence of the data hid the variations from public scrutiny. Second, the administrators in those institutions were probably not as firmly committed to reducing variations. The fact that they did not successfully implement MIS projects suggests that they were taking a less aggressive approach.

To summarize, institutions with MIS programs, especially those with advanced MIS, reduced the cost variations among departments. Explaining *why* this happened is much harder than simply stating that it did. The gaps among departments were probably reduced for a number of reasons, only one of which was the public information produced by an MIS. Administrative resolve, ceilings on expenditures, and pressure from boards of trustees were also parts of the equation. The management information systems were only one part of a complex puzzle.

Reduced Expenditures in Advanced MIS

Many institutions built MIS programs because they hoped that costs could be reduced with good information. Was that hope justified? All our information suggests that institutions with advanced MIS reduced costs, while those without these systems had constant increases. But we are *not* arguing that differences were due to the MIS projects *alone*. Let us examine the facts and then ask why the differences occurred.

The evidence on the cost question is in different tables. First, look back at Table 6. Over the four-year period from 1972 to 1976, the institutions with advanced MIS experienced the greatest declines in costs. (The sharp decrease in the "Too Early to Tell" category should be discounted because it is largely explained by unusual events in one institution.) By contrast, the largest *increase* occurred in those institutions that were least successful in implementing an MIS. Remember, the figures in Table 6 are in *constant* 1967 dollars.

The figures in Table 7 are in *current* dollars for each year. In this table, because of inflation, the prices of *all* institutions have increased. But again the pattern is obvious: the least successful institutions have the most increases, while the advanced MIS programs have the smallest increases. The findings in Tables 6 and 7 are highly consistent: Successful MIS programs are associated with reductions in costs. We need not jump to the conclusion that the MIS programs *caused* that reduction, but it is certainly an empirical fact that these programs *are associated* with reductions.

We decided to look even more closely at the pattern of cost reductions. Because of the time lag between the introduction of the system and the impact on costs, it seemed to us that a logical procedure would be to examine only those institutions that had had MIS for all four years. Table 8 shows data from only eight institutions. Six of those had had their MIS programs for all four years; two of the institutions had not had *any* program in the four years. By focusing on these eight institutions,

Table 7. Average Departmental Expenditures per FTE Student
(Current Dollars)
(23 Institutions with Exxon Grants
at Any Point During 4 Years)

Category of College	1972–73	1973–74	1974–75	1975–76	Average Annual Growth Rate, in Percentages	Average Growth for 4 Years, in Percentages
Least Successful (N = 35 depts.)						
Mean (X̄)	1,225	1,602	1,729	1,912	8	56
Standard Deviation	(648)	(493)	(458)	(649)		
Too Early to Tell[a] (N = 34 depts.)						
Mean (X̄)	912	819	909	939	1	3
Standard Deviation	(299)	(266)	(245)	(325)		
Successful Data-Bank MIS (N = 21 depts.)						
Mean (X̄)	1,475	1,505	1,797	1,809	5	23
Standard Deviation	(705)	(657)	(604)	(681)		
Successful Advanced MIS (N = 30 depts.)						
Mean (X̄)	1,814	1,847	1,830	1,986	5	9
Standard Deviation	(717)	(551)	(524)	(594)		
Successful MBO (with MIS) (N = 21 depts.)						
Mean (X̄)	1,001	996	1,035	1,124	4	12
Standard Deviation	(372)	(377)	(388)	(402)		
All Departments (N = 141)						
Average (X̄)	1,294	1,494	1,459	1,701	4	31
Standard Deviation	(570)	(475)	(443)	(546)		

Note: The pooled estimates are weighted averages of the estimates for different institutions. For each group, the estimates are obtained by weighting institutional averages by the number of departments at that institution.
[a]The decrease in this category is due to huge decreases in *one* institution. Without it the average annual rate would be .04 percent.

we expected to see the sharpest impact—the institutions with the longest time, contrasted with those that had no program. All other institutions fell somewhere in between on the time dimension and were excluded.

Does this "close-in" look demonstrate a high impact of the MIS programs on costs? Yes. Costs in institutions with advanced MIS programs remained constant (a 2 percent reduction), while all other institutions experienced sharp increases (roughly 25 percent). These figures are in current dollars; if we had used *constant* 1967 dollars, the institutions with advanced MIS would have shown an average 26 percent *decrease*, while the others would have remained almost level.

Early Implementation and Cost Reduction

We carried our analysis one step further, examining *early* implementation versus *late* implementation of MIS projects. (We confined this "time" analysis to advanced MIS projects only.) We were able to distinguish between institutions that implemented their systems in 1972–73 and those that implemented their systems later. Such a time breakdown is based on the assumption that there is a *lag* in the effect of these systems. For instance, a cost simulation model that is technically implemented in the 1972–73 academic year might be used in the 1973–74 fiscal year to assist in the allocation of resources in the 1974–75 year. There is probably at least a two-year lag between the implementation of these systems and their impact on departmental expenditures.

Table 9 describes the expenditures per FTE student for the sixty-one departments in the 1972–73 through 1975–76 academic years. Note that, on the average, departmental expenditures per FTE student increased in the four years. The one exception to this trend were those departments at institutions that implemented advanced MIS in 1972–73, the "early birds." Departmental expenditures per FTE student in these departments increased slightly through the 1974–75 academic year and then declined below the level of expenditures for the 1972–73 academic year. These results are further evidence that advanced MIS projects have an impact on the resources allocated to academic

Table 8. Departmental Expenditures per Student
(Current Dollars)
(8 Institutions with Full 4 Years in Program)

	1972–73	1973–74	1974–75	1975–76	Average Growth for 4 Years, in Percentages
No Information System					
Institution A ($N = 7$ depts.)					
Mean ($\bar{X}$)	764	731	893	839	10
Standard deviation	(209)	(319)	(300)	(361)	
Institution B ($N = 7$ depts.)					
Mean ($\bar{X}$)	1,282	1,305	1,605	1,693	32
Standard deviation	(472)	(460)	(507)	(492)	
Average of Institutions A and B					
Mean ($\bar{X}$)	1,034	1,018	1,249	1,265	24
Standard deviation	(365)	(395)	(416)	(431)	
Data-Bank MIS					
Institution C ($N = 7$ depts.)					
Mean ($\bar{X}$)	1,132	1,191	1,479	1,364	20
Standard deviation	(675)	(659)	(789)	(705)	
Institution D ($N = 7$ depts.)					
Mean ($\bar{X}$)	1,786	1,910	2,377	2,275	27
Standard deviation	(785)	(820)	(629)	(791)	

Institution E (N = 4 depts.)					
Mean (X̄)	838	996	997	1,071	29
Standard deviation	(199)	(257)	(149)	(387)	
Average of Institutions C, D, E					
Mean (X̄)	1,321	1,427	1,721	1,653	25
Standard deviation	(603)	(616)	(585)	(631)	
Advanced MIS					
Institution F (N = 3 depts.)					
Mean (X̄)	1,827	1,692	1,745	1,671	-9
Standard deviation	(647)	(593)	(481)	(588)	
Institution G (N = 6 depts.)					
Mean (X̄)	3,518	3,491	3,694	3,448	-2
Standard deviation	(1,326)	(924)	(991)	(532)	
Institution H (N = 7 depts.)					
Mean (X̄)	1,272	1,415	1,266	1,313	3
Standard deviation	(404)	(287)	(376)	(380)	
Average of Institutions F, G, H					
Mean (X̄)	2,218	2,245	2,275	2,180	-2
Standard deviation	(903)	(648)	(691)	(478)	

Table 9. Pooled Means and Standard Deviations
for Departmental Expenditures per FTE Student

	1972-73	1973-74	1974-75	1975-76
All Institutions (N = 61)				
Mean	1,594.96	1,698.20	1,796.83	1,854.06
Standard deviation	678.52	550.69	575.61	625.34
Unable to Implement (N = 21)				
Mean	1,259.16	1,485.75	1,535.33	1,726.03
Standard deviation	644.93	511.30	462.11	733.85
Late Implementation (N = 25)				
Mean	1,485.46	1,523.08	1,714.89	1,791.92
Standard deviation	509.52	521.02	450.59	543.59
Early Implementation (N = 15)				
Mean	2,247.60	2,287.53	2,299.54	2,136.94
Standard deviation	937.25	649.36	709.34	580.56

Note: The pooled estimates are weighted averages of the estimates for different institutions. For each group, the estimates are obtained by weighting institutional averages by the number of departments at that institution.

departments, with a typical two-year lag. The pooled standard deviations in Table 9 reinforce this conclusion. Colleges that implemented advanced MIS early in the game consistently reduced the cost variations between departments. Such shrinkage is evidence that these institutions are making selective adjustments.

Figure 1 is a graph of departmental expenditures per FTE student.* This graph illustrates that there are substantial differences in departmental expenditures per student among institutions. The graph also indicates that departmental expenditures per student were, on the average, increasing over those four years but that the early implementation institutions had the slowest growth rate.

*These trends were also analyzed by a three-way ANOVA with repeated measures. The results discussed in this section were found to be statistically significant in this analysis. The results are available upon request from the authors.

Figure 1. Departmental expenditures per FTE student, pooled mean.

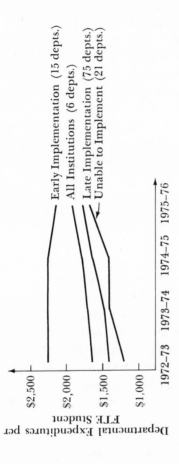

Strategies for Cost Reduction

The impact of advanced MIS on departmental expenditures per FTE student results from several fundamental policy changes, primarily those policies covering faculty compensation and student/faculty ratio.

Low Salary Increases. Table 10 shows the average faculty salary for the academic years 1972–73 through 1975–76. Faculty salaries have increased at an annual rate of a little over 3 percent per year, in current dollars. Compared with a typical year's increase in the consumer price index of 6.6 percent (and in several years much higher), the real value of faculty salaries declined in this period of high inflation. Faculty salaries, which were one of the major increases in educational expenditures during the 1960s' "golden years," are now one of the key methods used for reducing an institution's instructional costs.

Institutions that implemented advanced information systems in 1972–73 generally have the slowest rate of growth in average faculty salaries. One of these institutions estimated that each 1 percent increase in faculty compensation added $100,000 to institutional expenditures. Further, these increases are compounded because a salary increase in one year becomes the salary base for the following year's salary increase.

Increases in Student/Faculty Ratio. Instructional costs are determined by many factors, but the two most important are the number of students and faculty members. The student/faculty ratio is crucial in determining the costs for a department. Careful examination of our Exxon institutions showed that changing the student/faculty ratio was the single most important thing they did to control costs. We can summarize our findings in two statements.

First, institutions with no MIS or with data-bank MIS had mixed results: they had both declines and increases in the student/faculty ratio. Some departments increased the ratio, thus reducing expenditures per student. Generally, however, the student/faculty ratio declined slightly, from 5 percent to 10 percent over four years. This decline resulted in academic departments' becoming more expensive.

Second, institutions with advanced MIS were generally increasing the student/faculty ratio, averaging between 20 percent

Table 10. Average Faculty Salaries by Rank for Fiscal Years 1972–73 Through 1975–76 (Current Dollars)

Category of Institutions	1972–73	1973–74	1974–75	1975–76	Average Annual Growth Rates, in Percentages
All Institutions (N = 61)					
Full professors	22,718	24,156	25,479	26,948	4.4
Associate professors	17,378	18,175	19,123	20,258	3.9
Assistant professors	14,144	14,711	15,252	15,901	3.0
Instructors	11,370	12,054	12,570	13,013	3.4
Unable to Implement (N = 22)					
Full professors	21,757	23,151	24,568	26,327	4.9
Associate professors	17,680	18,537	19,272	20,910	4.2
Assistant professors	14,537	15,079	15,989	17,046	4.1
Instructors	11,779	12,698	13,044	13,573	3.6
Late Implementation (N = 25)					
Full professors	21,892	23,463	24,875	26,593	5.0
Associate professors	16,396	17,060	18,494	19,509	4.5
Assistant professors	13,127	13,398	14,244	15,053	3.5
Instructors	11,057	11,709	12,101	12,800	3.7
Early Implementation (N = 15)					
Full professors	24,186	25,519	26,690	27,717	3.5
Associate professors	18,160	19,050	19,655	20,574	3.2
Assistant professors	14,898	15,778	15,769	15,987	1.8
Instructors	11,410	11,971	12,723	12,852	3.1

and 40 percent increases over four years. This is the key conclusion: The institutions with advanced systems reduced their costs
because they reduced their prime instructional expense—faculty
salaries per student. Testimony from several institutions indicated that a *deliberate* policy decision, based partly on analyses
from the MIS, was made to increase the student/faculty ratio.
Obviously, one can increase this ratio by maintaining the current
level of enrollment and decreasing the size of the faculty (for
instance, by not filling faculty vacancies), or by increasing student enrollment while holding faculty size constant, or by some
combination of these strategies. The cost implications of the
alternatives are considerable. Wesleyan, for example, estimated
that decreasing the faculty size would reduce projected deficits
by $920,000 in the third year of a three-year project, while
increasing the number of students would reduce deficits by
$2,209,000 in the same period. Interviews at several institutions
suggested that a policy decision was made to opt for increasing
students precisely because of these financial implications.

The Wesleyan case is similar to the other institutions that
reduced costs by increasing the student/faculty ratio. Institutions generally achieved the reduction by increasing the number
of students, not by decreasing faculty size. The institutions with
advanced MIS projects averaged *increases* in students (in the
seven departments we examined) of 22 percent per department.
But the faculty in those departments remained essentially stable.
The result: decreased costs. By contrast, all other institutions
showed gradual—sometimes drastic—across-the-board erosions in
student enrollments in the departments we looked at. The typical *decline* was around 9 percent, but many departments had
much larger drops. At the same time, there were substantial cuts
in the number of faculty members—but the cuts were never as
large as the student enrollment decline. The result: student declines plunged faster than faculty declines, the student/faculty
ratio decreased, and the costs increased dramatically.

How Much Impact Did Advanced MIS Have?

There were fundamental changes in the resources allocated
to academic departments. How were these decisions reached,

and what role did management information systems play? To investigate these questions, we relied on institutional documents and the testimony of individual administrators.

The process by which Wesleyan University decided to increase its student/faculty ratio and reduce the rate of growth in faculty salaries was described in Chapter Three. The process was summarized by the associate treasurer as follows: "The procedure of issuing a series of administrative staff reports resulted in a participatory dialogue which involved all constituencies of the university. The staff reports provided a context for participation and reaction by faculty, students, alumni, trustees, and others. Thus, while the process was evolutionary and highly participatory, it did not represent decision making by committee. Ultimately, it was the responsibility of the senior administrative staff to frame a series of specific recommendations, to explain and defend them, and to project the implications—fiscal and otherwise—of their implementation."

Within the context of this process, the SEARCH model retained a low profile. Again quoting the associate treasurer, "While we are highly sensitive to process, particularly the participatory process, there is virtually no emphasis on the system qua system. If one were to ask a typical Wesleyan student or faculty member about long-range planning and budgetary practices, it is most likely that the 'Plan for Action' would be mentioned and highly unlikely that the SEARCH model or program budgeting, or any other management system, would come to mind. In all too many institutions, the preoccupation is with the planning and budgetary system as an entity per se, and not with the ends to which the system is but a means." However, the information provided by the SEARCH model helped the administrative staff frame a series of specific recommendations.

The Wesleyan model also helped administrators explain and defend their recommendations. Although faculty have always conceded that control of institutional finances is a valid exercise of administrative power, the information provided by these models tends to persuade faculty that such an exercise of power is proper. For instance, one officer (at another institution) stated: "RRPM was used to predict faculty needs and . . . to negotiate with the faculty chairmen. The chairmen [at first] resisted it and questioned its accuracy. However, we showed them that we [had] predicted their needs accurately, so that next year we had credibility and they used the information."

Two other institutions show how the student/faculty ratio was increased. Personal conversations with administrators at these two institutions indicate that the following circumstances were involved. Both institutions experienced a decline in enrollments in the early 1970s. While this pattern was not unusual for private liberal arts colleges, it resulted in substantial pressure from their respective boards to turn the situation around. By 1973–74 both of these institutions began to reverse the decline in enrollments. As enrollments increased, a top-level administrative decision was made to allow the student/faculty ratio to float up with the increasing enrollments. There was no widespread discussion of this decision (as there was at Wesleyan). It was simply made by two or three top administrators at these institutions. Such a decision process is not unusual in small, private liberal arts colleges.

We cannot determine the extent to which cost simulation models influenced these decisions. There was no computer modeling of this particular decision by either institution. When the decision was made to allow the student/faculty ratio to increase, these institutions did not precede this decision with an assessment of the long-range financial implications. Nevertheless, the MIS project may have produced some intangible benefits. Information provided by the MIS may have provided the basic framework in which this decision was reached. Administrators at these institutions certainly knew that increasing the student/faculty ratio would help, and the MIS projects certainly clarified that knowledge.

Were these intangible benefits worthwhile? In response to the question "Knowing what you know now and assuming *no outside funding*, would your institution have been justified in starting this project on its own?" seven administrators (64 percent) at one institution and two administrators (50 percent) at the other indicated that the benefits received were obtained at a reasonable cost. While explicit benefit-cost study would be extremely difficult, an administrator at one of these institutions reported:

> If one considered only the dollar investment in developing these programs versus the dollar return, it would not be difficult to prove that in one year this institution will recover its investment, and in two years it will recover an amount equal to the Exxon education grant and its own investment. But such return is not a full measure of success of such a program.
>
> Resource allocation programs are not merely for the present budget period but for guidance in future budget periods. Despite their enlightened environment, colleges are notoriously slow in changing to fit new conditions. Resource allocation programs can help to indicate desirable changes long before they have been made on a crisis basis. It is very difficult to put a dollar value on this contribution, but many faltering colleges would answer this by stating "What we would have given to have seen this coming."
>
> Nor can anyone place a dollar sign on readily available, accurate, and complete data. . . . Such data make it easier to provide information required for private, state, and national agencies and to make internal studies with speed and confidence.

Summary

We want to be cautious in our conclusions about the overall financial impacts. Remember, only about half the institutions in the Exxon study provided us with proper data. And to ensure comparability of departments, we focused on seven; we do not know what was happening in the other departments. To add to our list of problems, only about three institutions had the full impact of advanced MIS for four complete years in the Exxon program. In addition, the most important reservation is that many other things happened in these institutions while the Exxon grants were working. New administrators came on the scene, student enrollments leveled off, the rate of inflation rose dramatically, and the government's role in student aid changed significantly. In short, there was a buzzing, booming confusion going on.

Given these limitations, any conclusions we have reached should be considered with care. It would be ridiculous to claim that the changes we have noted are due entirely to the introduction of management information systems. A more likely explanation is that the management information systems *helped* with changes that were going to occur anyway. Aggressive administrators had made up their minds that they were going to reduce costs; they looked around for a tool to help them do it. They seized on the management information system as an appropriate mechanism. The lesson is important: introducing the management information system is only one small piece of the puzzle; to control costs, a determined effort must be made in a variety of areas. However, we do not want to *underestimate* the contributions of the MIS programs. Although they certainly did not singlehandedly reduce the costs, they nevertheless were one important ingredient in a complex situation. The systems provided two crucial things: reliable data and the ability to predict alternative consequences of decisions.

Wesleyan, for instance, simulated the financial implications of sixteen different ways to change its student/faculty ratio. These alternatives involved increasing enrollment by 100 to as many as 450 students, and reducing faculty size by 5 to 40 members. The college eventually decided to increase enrollments by 100 and to reduce the number of faculty members by 40. This combination was selected primarily because of the need to increase capital expenditures if enrollments were allowed to increase beyond 100 students and because this reduction could be accomplished through "orderly attrition."

In short, the information provided by these systems can influence decision makers to select different alternatives. Actually, these systems probably provide little new information. Few administrators would be surprised to find that increasing the student/faculty ratio would increase student revenues and reduce instructional expenditures. However, the ability to compare alternative ways of increasing this ratio may influence an administrator to select one method over another. This capability, limited in manual systems, is greatly enhanced by MIS.

MIS alone, then, could hardly account for the large changes in departmental costs. But good data and the ability to manipulate them were major advantages for aggressive administrations trying to cut costs. The reduction in costs in institutions with advanced MIS projects was probably due to a number of fortunate factors, including aggressive administrations, wealthy endowments, and a large pool of students who would increase the enrollment any time the administration desired. The other institutions were less wealthy, less prestigious, and had a smaller student pool from which they could draw. Needless to say, these environmental factors—not whether an institution had a good data system—often made the crucial difference. Nevertheless, the data systems were a bonus that reinforced the other advantages of these selective institutions.

Chapter Seven

Weighing the Managerial and Institutional Impact

The Exxon Education Foundation funded these projects to promote efficient planning, cost-effective budgeting, and better administrative behavior. Were those benefits accomplished by the various projects? Most of our research tried to answer these questions in one way or another:

1. Was the data base for making decisions improved?
2. Did the planning process change? If so, in what ways? Were some areas affected more than others?
3. How did the faculty react to these managerial changes? Did the faculty members consider the changes appropriate and legitimate? Did the changes influence the morale of the faculty?
4. Were there any side effects or unintended results? If so, which of them were positive and which negative?

5. Did significant problems emerge? Were there important lessons to be learned from the projects?

Improvements in the Data Base

Most projects tried to improve the data base for decision making. The more successful projects seemed to translate those initial good intentions into reality. Their data bases did improve significantly, if we are to believe our respondents.

First of all, *the quality of the data improved*. In Table 11 Questions 1, 2, and 3 concern improvements in the data base. Several patterns emerged. First, the institutions that combined a data base with a "simulation" capacity or a management by objectives program showed significantly greater improvement than the other institutions. In a few cases, there were dramatically high levels of improvements. Second, data about students and their patterns of enrollment improved much more than any other data. This result is consistent with the intention of most data systems; since they are "student driven," the whole system is based on enrollment patterns. Third, the six institutions with "simple data banks" had an unusual split in their results. They showed strong improvements in their student data but relatively weak improvements in their faculty data and financial data. In these institutions, the real focus seemed to be in improving the student data. Probably, as simple systems add the ability to simulate and model decisions, they also improve the data on faculty and finances. The student data are the base; more sophisticated systems gradually add frosting to the cake.

In addition, the speed of problem solving often increased. In institutions where the management information system was able to develop a solid data base and the software to process it, decisions often were made much more quickly. The dean of instruction at a small New England college told us: "I really don't feel like our new MIS told us anything we didn't already know. Every college is probably like ours. There is somebody stationed somewhere in the bowels of the organization that keeps up with the statistics. Every college has its old Mrs. Jones or old Mr. Smith, who has been around for years, collects up all the data,

Table 11. Percent of Administrators Agreeing with Questions in Different Categories of Colleges

	Category of College					
	Least Successful	Too Early to Tell	Successful Data-Bank MIS	Successful Advanced MIS	Successful MBO (with MIS)	
1. Overall improvement in student data	41	58	65	66	81	
2. Overall improvement in faculty data	25	48	22	50	62	
3. Overall improvement in financial data	33	52	36	53	62	
4. Institutional forecasts and long-range planning improved	42	35	63	67	85	
5. Overall improvement in setting objectives	38	54	52	49	80	
6. Overall improvement in implementing goal attainment	33	36	39	40	83	
7. Overall improvement in assessing goal attainment	26	32	45	44	70	
8. Overall improvement in curriculum planning	29	32	40	45	50	
9. Overall improvement in allocating faculty positions	28	28	21	43	56	
10. Budgetary and faculty allocation decisions are more centralized	22	5	20	17	14	
11. Budgetary and faculty allocation decisions decentralized to department chairpersons	4	5	9	29	44	
12. Overall improvement in budget process	33	47	32	61	80	

and every so often makes a report. So in one sense we've had the data for as long as I can remember. But with the new MIS we can get the data *faster*, we can get *more* data when we need it. We can cover a *broader spectrum* of issues in the same amount of time. We always had the potential to get the data eventually; but now we can get it when we need it. I think that's the real breakthrough. The improvement is a timing question." This dean's comments were supported by most people in institutions with successful projects. However, there was some tendency in the opposite direction. In some institutions where the projects got stalled, a major complaint concerned timing. In MIS programs, the data were not available when the decision makers needed them; in an MBO process, the planning cycle did not mesh with the budgeting process.

Another problem that plagued both the successful and the unsuccessful institutions was the "junk" issue. Some projects furnished entirely too much unfocused data, tons of junk with no point of concentration. Sometimes it actually took the administrators *longer* to sort through the printout and make decisions. This complaint arose many times. The decision process can actually be slowed down by data if they are not focused and condensed.

The timing has to be delicately balanced. On the one hand, computers can provide more information quickly. If that information is focused, condensed, and directed toward concrete decisions, it can speed up the decision-making process. On the other hand, some systems deliver reams of printout with little focus and a high degree of "noise." This deluge is likely to slow down the process while the decision makers plow through the pages. The administrators have to stop and translate the raw data into "information" that they can use. Timing, then, is a delicate matter and can easily tip decision making in either direction.

Good data also facilitated "hot-spot analysis." The president of a small religious college in the South framed this issue: "Having these data allows me to do overall planning better. But one of the features I like best is that it also allows me to move in the other direction—focus very narrowly on the 'hot spots.' By 'hot-spot analysis' I mean I can see small problems in the data that are sure to grow bigger. By isolating some of these hot spots, I can usually catch some problems before they go too far. Of course, if I had known the right question, I would have been able to get this information without the MIS. But that's just the point—the system sometimes spotlights issues that I never would have dreamed to ask about. When these hot spots jump up, they almost call attention to themselves. In my opinion, this is one of the most valuable aspects of our data system." That interview came early in our research. Subsequently, when we were interviewing at other colleges, we asked people whether they had similar experiences. Most people could immediately identify with the notion of "hot-spot analysis." In fact, they usually had an illustration of a problem that jumped out of the data at their college. For example:

1. At Furman University in South Carolina, the data system put the spotlight on gift income. In previous years the college had budgeted its *guesses* about gift income. Later, if the gift income fell short or ran ahead, the budget had to be adjusted. Consequently, extreme fluctuations in the gift income showed up in the data. Someone suggested that this was causing many problems in the budgeting process. So Furman decided to skip one year's gift income and bank it, then budget the next year on the past year's gift income. By this technique the institution was able to predict with a high degree of accuracy the budget implications of gift income. Although anyone could have suggested this strategy before the college had the data system, the data system pinpointed the problem. Once it was recognized, the strategy was undertaken.

2. At Mount Saint Mary's College in Los Angeles, the dean of instruction showed us the latest computer runs on faculty/ student ratios in various departments. Having these data in usable form, she said, helped her see more accurately the extremely high cost some departments incurred because of low student/ faculty ratios. She had always intuitively known this, but the hard data spotlighted the problem. As a consequence, she took action to help those departments attract more students and eliminate duplicate courses with small enrollments.

3. At West Virginia Wesleyan College, the "hot-spot analysis" focused on recruiting patterns. West Virginia Wesleyan had

been experiencing a sharp drop in enrollment. It undertook a strong campaign to recruit more students. The new data system, however, showed that much effort was going into recruiting programs for students in extremely expensive fields. A computer printout on the recruiting costs in different fields suggested that, in some ways, the university was defeating its purpose. It was often spending recruiting money on exactly the students who were going to cost the institution more money. And it was sometimes neglecting fields where students could be educated for a smaller investment. In addition, the hot-spot analysis helped the college focus carefully on the high school districts from which many students were already coming to Wesleyan. Armed with this information, Wesleyan began a concentrated recruiting effort in the most promising high school districts, rather than scattering its efforts all over its region. Using this strategy, which had evolved partly from a hot-spot analysis of the data, Wesleyan was able to reverse its enrollment pattern dramatically. The enrollment completely turned around in a two-year period, and the institution is now growing.

Time and again during our interviews, people pointed out examples where the data had highlighted issues that had previously been neglected. It was not that the data were unavailable; it was simply that they had not become salient in anybody's mind. They had never "jumped out" so that anyone paid attention to them. One major advantage of a good management information system is this ability to spotlight special problems. Although these systems are most likely to cause spotlighting, the same focused attention sometimes occurs during the process of planning in an MBO project.

Improvements in the Planning Process

A prime objective in the Exxon program was to improve the planning process at colleges. Consequently, in our questionnaires and interviews, we concentrated much attention on the planning process.

Question 4 in Table 11 shows the percentage of administrators who felt that long-range planning had been improved as a result of the Exxon project. There are some strong conclusions from the data. First, the institutions with a combined MIS/MBO program had a very high level of people who felt there was improvement—85 percent. The management by objectives programs were *intended* to improve the planning process. If the administrators were responding accurately to this question, that intention was certainly translated into reality. In institutions where the management by objectives program had been uniquely successful—for example, at Furman University, Arkansas College, and Earlham College—people felt that there was an entirely new focus on institutional planning. Large numbers of faculty members and administrators worked together to produce departmental plans and institutional guidelines.

The second obvious result from Question 4 is that the two types of management information systems also significantly improved planning, although not as much as the combined MIS/MBO projects. Approximately two thirds of the administrators in the successful MIS colleges felt that institutional forecasts and long-range planning had improved. This percentage stands in sharp contrast to that of institutions that were "least successful" and "too early to tell." In those institutions, roughly one third of the people felt that there had been improvement.

The data in Table 11 came only from administrators. We wondered whether the faculty were also as optimistic about the improvements in planning. Consequently, we examined another survey that included faculty. Table 12 shows the administrator and faculty responses from that survey. As the table indicates, institutions with successful projects show more improvement in planning than those with unsuccessful projects; the differences, however, are not sharp. Moreover, in almost every case, regardless of the category of institution, the faculty members are not as optimistic as the administrators.

Why does the administrative questionnaire suggest much improvement in planning whereas the administrative-faculty questionnaire shows less improvement? We suspect a double-edged sword. First, the administrators were answering a questionnaire *specifically* about the Exxon projects. Since they were closest to the project, they were more likely to see the improvement. Also, they were more likely to have a vested interest in

Table 12. Attention to Planning
(Higher Score = More Planning Activity)
(N = 34)

Type of Project		Mean Score[a]
Least Successful	Everybody combined	2.54/2.52
N = 9	Administrators only	2.53/2.55
	Faculty only	2.55/2.15
Too Early to Tell	Everybody combined	2.74/2.75
N = 8	Administrators only	2.83/2.79
	Faculty only	2.64/2.72
Successful	Everybody combined	2.86/2.85
Data-Bank MIS	Administrators only	2.90/2.89
N = 4	Faculty only	2.48/2.59
Successful	Everybody combined	2.77/2.72
Advanced MIS	Administrators only	2.81/2.80
N = 7	Faculty only	2.60/2.47
Successful MBO	Everybody combined	2.80/2.75
(with MIS)	Administrators only	2.85/2.81
N = 6	Faculty only	2.67/2.57

Note: This questionnaire contained many items about planning in the college. The different questions were combined to obtain a scale score (1 = no planning, 4 = much planning). Roughly, the higher the score, the more managerial planning the respondents perceived.
[a] Two scores are given for each entry. The first score was obtained at the beginning of the project; the second score, near the end of the project.

wanting to make the project look successful. By contrast, since these were management innovations, the faculty was less likely to be close to the projects and to have a vested interest in making the projects look good. To summarize, then, the administrators saw sharp improvement in planning, and the faculties at the successful institutions agreed—at least to some extent.

There was an increase in the general sophistication about problems. We have noted that one advantage of a good data system is the ability to spotlight problems, to do a hot-spot analysis. At the other extreme, however, the successful systems also seemed to build a generalized sophistication about problems. In our interviews, faculty members often commented that they now understood more of the implications of the empirical data. They often argued over those data, pointed out how "biased" they were, or challenged the assumptions behind them. Nevertheless, even in rejecting unfavorable data, faculty members were educated to the problems that administrators faced. For example, we heard faculty members say that for the first time they really understood how expensive some departments were, compared with others, or how students were distributed within departments. Most important, many faculty members commented that for the first time they really understood the *interdependency* among departments. The English department, for example, was teaching a large number of business school students, and without them many English professors would be unemployed.

The planning cycles in an MBO project also fostered this general sophistication about institutional problems. The planning within each department promoted discussions about departmental goals and objectives that might never have occurred otherwise. As those discussions moved forward, the general awareness about departmental problems increased. The same thing happened as those departmental plans were passed to higher levels. Then department heads had to discuss their plans in conjunction with other department heads and deans. This sharing of perspectives helped educate everyone to the interdependencies among departments. The special problems and unique concerns of different departments were shared. The president of one college in extreme financial difficulty summed up the matter: "The most important benefit of our MIS program, and the MBO program that went with it, was the increase in everybody's general awareness of the problems we face—faculty, trustees, and administrators alike. The planning that accompanies this project made us all realize we were on the same ship. And if it sank, we were all going to drown. Rivalries didn't disappear overnight, and the data didn't eliminate all conflict. But people understood each other's problems better. An overall 'institutional perspective' developed to help balance the provincial perspectives of the different departments. The general fund of information about problems has gone up around here."

A side effect of this increased sophistication is the increased legitimacy of decisions. Although not everybody agreed that the legitimacy of decisions had increased, a number of faculty members told us: "We don't necessarily agree with the decisions, but after all the facts are presented, we at least understand the problems better. The decisions seem much fairer."

To complicate matters, many economic problems for higher education occurred almost simultaneously with the introduction of these projects. We anticipated much improvement in faculty attitudes toward administrators as a result of these projects. But that anticipated improvement was clouded by the hard decisions required during the economic crisis. These projects may have increased the legitimacy of decisions, but struggles over the economic crisis probably decreased faculty trust in the administration. So it is difficult to determine what was going on.

From our interviews, at least, we felt that well-organized projects, particularly the MBO projects, built a greater sense of legitimacy about decisions and confidence toward the administrators. However, controversies over the economic crisis probably balanced the process and undermined some of the positive aspects of the projects. We can only speculate, but in an economic crisis faculty feelings of distrust toward administrators who were making unpopular decisions might have been even worse if it had not been for the projects.

The MBO programs had unique strengths in improving the planning process. We have been talking until now about MIS and MBO together. Both types of projects had favorable impacts on the data base and on the planning process. However, the MBO projects seemed to have a uniquely strong impact on the planning process. As we noted in Chapter Four, there were no "pure" types of MBO projects; every management by objectives project also had a strong data base and was coupled with an MIS. In a sense, then, these projects used a basic MIS *plus* an MBO effort.

When the MIS and the MBO were combined, the improvement of planning seemed dramatic. Examine Questions 5, 6, and 7 in Table 11. On each question, the combined MIS/MBO group is significantly higher than any other type of project—usually twice as high. Eighty percent of administrators in those institutions with combined projects felt that there was an improvement in setting objectives; 83 percent saw an improvement in implementing goal attainment; 70 percent saw an improvement in assessing goal attainment. We also mentioned earlier that 85 percent of the administrators in institutions with combined MIS/MBO projects saw improvements in the long-range planning process (Question 4). It is obvious that the combined MBO/MIS projects concentrated on the planning process, and they had substantial success.

This leads us to one of the most important conclusions in this study. From the research we have done, *we believe that one of the most powerful managerial innovations is a strong data-based MIS linked to a vigorous management by objectives program.* This is a sharp change from our initial opinions. When we began this study, some staff members were frankly doubtful about the impacts of the management by objectives projects. At the end of the study, however, we were highly impressed with the value of the MBO projects. They were particularly powerful in improving the planning processes and, when linked to an MIS, also captured most of the positive effects that the MIS offers. In fact, we were somewhat surprised that the combined MIS/MBO was able to do both tasks well: to improve planning (the major thrust of the MBO strategy) while simultaneously improving the data base (the major thrust of the MIS projects). When we look at Table 11, it is surprising how often the combined MIS/MBO institutions had the highest improvement on almost every question. In short, our research team was very impressed with the positive benefits from coupling both types of management innovations.

Unanticipated Consequences

We have discussed the intended outcomes of the projects. Now let us examine some of their *unanticipated* and *unplanned* consequences. Often there were subtle shifts in decision making or minor adjustments in power relationships that nobody really planned. Management innovations, particularly MIS projects, are usually designed to make more effective use of campus resources. They are often financial-planning systems. These systems may, however, establish new rules that will affect behavior of academic departments in general and departmental chairpersons in particular. Specifically, new rules for calculating work loads and for assigning costs may produce incentives to maximize enrollments while limiting the costs assigned to the department. Let us look at this unanticipated consequence.

   The adoption of MIS will cause departments to maximize enrollments. An MIS usually ties faculty positions and other resources directly to the number of student credit hours generated by a department. The commonsense notion is obvious: more students, more money. Of course, it did not take sophisticated computers to promote this old-fashioned logic; every department head in the nation has always known and practiced this strategy. The careful statistics of an MIS, however, raise the simple logic to a relentless science. Now the simple logic is augmented by computer printouts that spin out the facts in minute detail, that highlight—in public—departmental weaknesses, that chronicle failures for the scrutiny of everyone who can read, that compile the dismal statistics year after year in neat columns. The commonsense equation between students and money is multiplied many times over with an MIS, especially in a time of financial crisis. Thus, if the department is to increase its academic program, it must increase the number of students who enroll in the department.

   Academic departments may increase their level of student enrollments in at least four ways. First, departments may *add new courses* to attract more students, or at least maintain their current level of enrollment. A public posture of "relevance" may, in fact, be an attempt to play on the current curricular fads of students. In some cases, the development of new courses results from a calculated study of the market. For example, at Adelphi University the School of Business Administration developed its EDUTRAIN, a rail car on which commuters between Long Island and New York City can work toward an MBA degree while commuting. On the West Coast, a number of public and private institutions have been expanding nursing programs, a sure-fire growth area. The rash of new off-campus extension and special-degree programs is a symptom of student chasing evident all over the nation. A second way to increase enrollments is to *eliminate courses* that have few students. If the rule for allocating faculty positions to a department requires an average class size of fifteen students, courses with more than fifteen students are subsidizing courses with fewer. Most departments are willing to accept lower-division subsidizing of upper-division courses. However, certain lower-division courses may not have enough students. Thus, a department may cancel one course in the hope that a more attractive course can be substituted. The traditional enrollment booster is to *require students to take certain courses*. There is probably no faster way to increase students in foreign language departments, for example, than to impose a five-course foreign language requirement—and no faster way to decrease student demand than to drop such a course requirement. Finally, the use of an MIS provides a clue to yet another way in which academic departments may increase students: the fact that students enroll in courses outside their major fields points to *interdependencies among academic departments*. For instance, an increase in the number of students in a college's nursing program will increase the number of students in biology courses. Generally, department chairpersons have seen the allocation of available faculty positions and any allocation of an additional faculty position to one department comes at the expense of another department. But a clever biology department chairperson would welcome efforts by the nursing program to expand, knowing that the department would be the beneficiary of some student "fallout."

Departments will try to minimize the indirect costs assigned to them. Sometimes administrators will use an MIS to assign "indirect" costs—for example, libraries, counseling services, computer center—to the users of those services. This procedure of "charging back" the cost is intended to assist campus decision makers in anticipating the total costs of operating each academic department. However, these procedures may lead to defensive behavior by the departments, to hide or reduce the charges assigned to them. These defensive actions may hurt the academic program.

One type of dysfunctional behavior is to *drop support services*. For instance, if an academic department is charged for the counseling services used by its student majors, that department may discourage its students from obtaining counseling. Although the indirect costs assigned to the department would be decreased, the number of students who might need the services would remain the same. Costs would be lower, but the services delivered to students would be fewer. Other harmful cuts can be imagined: in library acquisitions, laboratory usage, or computer time available for instruction. A second unfortunate side effect might be an increase in *departmental distrust* and lack of cooperation as a result of full costing. Because departments are charged for services over which they have little, if any, control, the situation is ripe for complaints that unfair charges are made against the department's accounts. The resultant bickering between departments and administration may detract from the effectiveness of full-costing procedures.

In some instances—most notably when the services are highly valued and the allocation is based on prior usage patterns—departments will try to maximize total indirect costs. At the University of California at Los Angeles, for example, the allocation of computer funds for instructional purposes is based on the total expenditures for computer services during the previous year. Such a procedure motivates potential users to request more computer funds than they can actually use wisely and to spend all the funds prior to the end of the fiscal year, even if funds are squandered. This kind of behavior is another unanticipated consequence of an MIS.

These unexpected consequences are not always negative, however. Strong management information systems can have some very positive but unplanned impacts on departmental management. Many of the pitfalls outlined above can be avoided if wise use is made of these information systems. For example, Furman University has developed an integrated management system composed of an institutional research office, an information system, and organizational development strategies. By using information distributed to departments, and by involving the departments heavily in the planning process, Furman has been able to develop a participative management system.

Effects on Centralization of Authority

The literature on academic management usually stresses the importance of decentralization, of placing effective decision making at the lowest possible level. In fact, the call for decentralization has almost assumed the position of a dogma, a truth that is simply assumed. But the issue may be substantially more complex; decentralization may be a benefit under some circumstances and a disaster under others. Some features about colleges and universities make decentralization desirable: (1) the importance of professionals participating in decisions; (2) the increase in morale that comes from "owning" a decision and participating in it; (3) the highly fragmented nature of academic departments that have special needs and want close-to-home management; and (4) the desire to get decisions closer to the departmental homes of students, so that they can participate. On the other side of the coin, however, some factors limit the usefulness of decentralization: (1) a financial crisis that calls for maximum efficiency and coordination in using money; (2) a provincialism in academic departments which could undermine overall institutional needs; (3) an orientation by department chairpersons toward the department instead of the whole institution; (4) an inability of central administration to reward department chairs or to evaluate their performance effectively; (5) a growing movement toward faculty collective bargaining, with a resultant polarization that undercuts the "collegial" atmosphere, in which decentralization supposedly works better.

In short, the desirability of decentralization is a complex issue that depends heavily on financial conditions and organizational needs. But what impact do management information systems and MBO projects have on the centralization issue? They probably have different effects, so let us examine them separately.

MIS projects will probably increase centralization. That is, in an "information-poor" organization such as a college or university, information can have a substantial effect on the distribution of power (see Cohen and March, 1974). First, the bulk of the information provided by MIS networks is in the hands of campus administrators. Second, administrators can devote considerable time to studying this information. In colleges, as in other organizations, time is a scarce resource. For the most part, faculty members have little time to study the operation of various departments. Consequently, administrators' are able to develop substantial and unopposed expertise in important areas.

Third, the new information produced by MIS programs some-times allows administrators to select changes that have "high leverage" but "low political salience" for the campus commu-nity. By careful use of the data, a shrewd administrator can fer-ret out issues that have high impact but are not directly in the arena of political concern. For example, the provost of one pres-tigious institution said that the most important thing he had done in ten years was to change the "indirect cost" charge in federal and foundation grants. This measure caused only a little controversy, confined to a small group of researchers, but the change produced substantially greater income for the university. Other examples of "high leverage/low political saliency" issues can be found. For example, minor variations in overall student/ faculty ratios can produce substantial savings, especially if a few students are added instead of some faculty members cut. Or shifts in recruitment emphasis can bring in more students in less expensive programs. Or a change in computer-time allocation can favor departments that use computer facilities effectively. In sum, a good MIS can provide an attentive administrator many opportunities to gain influence over high leverage/low political issues.

Centralization of power, then, might increase in colleges that adopt MIS programs. But what happens with the MBO pro-jects, where one of the specific intentions is to decentralize in-fluence? In Table 11 we see some interesting patterns in Questions 10 and 11. The first conclusion from the answer to Question 10 is that many administrators—roughly one fifth—felt that there was more centralization of authority. However, the largest per-centage of administrators who saw more centralization were in institutions where the projects were *least* successful. This was counter to our original assumption that the more successful MIS projects would tend to centralize power. The explanation is probably in the next question. A large percentage (44 percent) of the administrators in institutions with successful MBO pro-jects felt that budgetary and faculty allocation decisions had been decentralized to the department chairpersons. And 29 percent of the administrators in institutions with advanced MIS felt the same way. By contrast, only a handful of administrators in other institutions agreed that power had been decentralized.

What is going on here? First, our assumption that power would be more centralized has been partly supported and partly challenged by the data. Although the MIS projects have mixed results, the successful MBO projects seem to decentralize power, to involve the department chairpersons more in planning, and to give more people a sense of "owning" the decisions. We were pleasantly surprised at that finding. The other part of our explanation is even simpler: the administrators are being overoptimistic about how much power is being decentralized to department chairpersons. Remember, department chairpersons were not included in this survey. In another similar survey, when we asked department chairpersons about power, we found no change whatsoever in the perception of centralization. In summary, then, we feel that two things are happening. First, there may actually be some decentralization with these projects, especially the MBO types. But, second, much of the decentralization perceived by top administrators is simply wishful thinking, and the department chairpersons do not agree.

In addition, we still believe that centralization has actually increased, because of our vivid memories of interviews with people who insisted that there had been increased centralization. Again, the interviews had the same split; more people in the institutions with MIS programs believed that there had been centralization than in those with MBO programs. Clearly, this makes sense, because our beliefs about increased centralization were largely directed toward the MIS programs in the first place. And, by contrast, the MBO programs were deliberately designed to promote decentralization.

To sum up this complex issue:

1. There is probably more centralization of power in institutions that have implemented MIS projects.
2. The centralization caused by the MIS projects is reinforced by the financial crisis, which also promotes centralization.
3. However, that centralization was not nearly as strong as we had anticipated.
4. In particular, the MBO programs seemed to be uniquely successful in avoiding centralization. In fact, many administrators

on campuses with MBO projects actually felt that there had been a decentralization of power.

An Unresolved Problem: Linking Planning and Budgets

We are convinced that the project impacts could have been increased substantially if the planning process and the budgeting process had been more closely linked. We have seen that the projects that combined an MIS and an MBO seemed to have the most positive impacts. We think that a threefold combination would have been even better: a strong data base, a solid planning program under an MBO project, and a budgeting cycle that linked both together.

A few projects were related to the budgeting process. In nearly all cases, the data collected for an MIS were used in the budgeting process. There were many positive impacts on the budgeting process: priorities were clearer, the "hot-spot analysis" helped highlight problems in the budget, the interdependency between departments was clearer, budget decisions affecting one department were expanded to consider other departments. So, in some ways, the MIS projects did tie the planning process to the budgeting process by providing a data base on which to make decisions.

By contrast, in only a few cases was the MBO program directly linked to the budgeting process. In one such case, Arkansas College, many people felt that there had been a dramatic improvement in both the planning and the budgeting processes. Plans cannot be made in a vacuum. To plan with one hand and budget with the other is to invite suicide—or, at the very least, gross inefficiency. Most important, people want to believe that their plans are somehow going to influence budgeting decisions. They become disillusioned when there is no such influence. In our interviews, a number of department chairpersons felt that they had participated in a make-believe planning process that was never linked with budgeting. A link between planning and budgeting is critical for efficient planning; it is also essential for the morale of people doing the planning.

This does not mean that "wish lists" constructed during

planning must dictate the budget. In fact, the real world of the budget must be considered at every point. We believe that the process actually works in the other direction. When budget realities are known, they can have a sobering effect on the people doing the planning. Consequently, people are more likely to abandon their wish lists and design realistic, cost-conscious plans.

We would like to stress this point strongly. Earlier we said that coupling a strong MBO program with an MIS program was one of our most important recommendations. Let us add a second: *The planning process must be linked with the budgeting process.* Without that linkage, the planning process is nothing more than a sham in which people spend time and energy but become extremely disillusioned. Budgets are useful only when they implement serious plans. The planning process is sensible only when it can be linked to real-world budgets. This can be a threatening enterprise for administrators who have traditionally held the reins over the budget. It is one thing to let faculty members and department heads go off and plan—"to play games in the sand box," as one president cynically noted. It is quite another thing to involve the faculty, department heads, and deans in a serious planning exercise that has real-life financial consequences. This probably means that conflict will also increase. Planning in a vacuum usually does not cause conflict; make-believe play rarely does. But when the planning is connected with the budget, the conflict level will surely rise. Thus, administrators can be threatened by a double-edged sword: a need to share power and an increase in conflict. Nevertheless, we believe that, in the real world of management and administration, shared power and conflict over resources have to be handled rather than hidden. We stress once again that linking the planning process, the data-gathering process, and the budgeting system is absolutely essential.

Chapter Eight

Implementing Managerial Innovations Successfully

One of our major concerns in this study was to determine which factors would support managerial innovations and which would undermine them. As we explained earlier, some of the projects were very successful, but others failed completely. Why were some innovations strong and healthy, and others so weak that they died?

There were some notable patterns. In the more successful projects, administrative support was firm, funding was generous, the project directors had excellent skills, and faculty support was strong. By contrast, other projects were often cut loose and left adrift. They had little administrative support and faced outright antagonism by the faculties.

From our interview and questionnaires at various stages of the project, we were able to assemble a picture of the forces that supported or undermined the process. Different pieces of advice are relevant to different stages in the project. We examined the "life cycle" of a project and analyzed administrative practices that supported the projects in each phase. The life-cycle notion is simple: There are activities necessary to support a project during its *initiation*, during its struggling *early period*, during its *mature period* of routine operation, and even in those waning days of *project death*. We will explore some rules for supporting innovations at various phases of a project's life cycle.

Project-Initiation Period

How does a project get started in the first place? In theory, an innovation is introduced because of some serious need in the institution. Also in theory, administrators study their organization and then carefully determine strategies to solve the institutional problems. In reality, however, serious problem assessment is not always the stimulus for a management innovation. Sometimes managerial innovations come from an administrator's ego need to prove that he is "innovative"; from "grant chasing," where an institution simply goes after available money regardless of its needs; from consultants imposing their "bag of tricks" on the institution; or from people insisting on change that meets their narrow needs. Let us look at some rules about initiating innovations in the managerial areas.

Innovations must be responsive to real organizational needs. Why does this college need some managerial innovation? Will a management by objectives program have anything to offer? What real managerial needs will be met by introducing some new program? Often these questions are not clearly answered before a management innovation is initiated. It seems simpleminded to say that needs assessment should precede the innovation. But in all too many situations, no serious assessment of institutional problems is undertaken. Instead, managerial innovations are picked up and used just because they are available, because granting agencies provide funds, or because other institutions are "doing it." What factors block adequate needs assessment?

First, there is the problem of *back-pocket solutions*. Administrators frequently develop their own pat diagnosis of organizational needs. People may have axes to grind, or they may have picked up an idea from the literature or from a friend. Then, with the best of intentions, they apply their back-pocket solution to every problem that arises, even if the problem does not need that particular solution. The old saying certainly holds true: "Give a little boy a hammer and suddenly the whole world needs to be hammered."

Usually, administrators will adopt some preconceived solution within their own span of control and close to the power levers they can pull. This is not necessarily bad; we all have a tendency to specialize and concentrate in our own sphere of activity. However, applying ready-made solutions within our power domain may lead to a persistent bias and to a systematic neglect of the whole organization's needs. In some of the institutions with grants from the Exxon Education Foundation, this tendency was pronounced. Sometimes an administrator would grab a management information system because he had read about it or because a friend in another institution was using it. In many cases, there was no systematic analysis of whether a management information system would really solve the problem. There was an unfortunate tendency to jump at these innovations without really evaluating the potential outcome. The back-pocket solution was applied without much thought.

The second problem that short-circuits serious needs assessment is the *iceberg phenomenon*. This is a tendency to do some superficial needs assessment but never dig deep enough to get at the real problem. For example, one college that received an Exxon grant—and later let the project die completely—had a faculty committee studying budget reductions. This committee began to search for a data-analysis technique, such as a management information system, because data needed in budgeting were unavailable. The committee did not realize, however, that the problem was an almost complete breakdown between the department chairpersons and the higher administration. The lack of information was *not* due to unsophisticated data handling; it was due to a *deliberate policy* by the department chairpersons to hide information from both faculty committees and the president.

The tip of the iceberg—the lack of information—was showing. But the real problem—the lack of trust—was never openly discussed, because the department chairpersons felt that any information they supplied would be used to cut their budgets. In this particular case, if the faculty committee had gone below the surface, it would have seen that any management information system would have to be supported by an attempt to win the confidence and support of the department chairpersons. Because this deeper task was never undertaken, the project was a complete failure. Unfortunately, people have a tendency to short-circuit their needs assessment and to address themselves only to the superficial aspects.

A third reason that needs assessment is often short-circuited is mindless *grant chasing*. The stimulus for a management innovation is often some outside offer of funding. Our interviews revealed that, in many cases, there had been little needs assessment before the Exxon institutions applied for grants. The real stimulus was simply the available money. As one cynical department chairperson told us, "Our president is a grant whore; he'll take anything as long as he can grab some money. And he doesn't give a damn whether we really need it!" Thoughtless grant chasing seems to be a source of many failures. Since there is no real connection to institutional needs, the project lives only as long as the outside money is available.

Watch for consultants with their bags of tricks. Outside consultants often play a critical role in the initial phase of a management innovation project. In many cases, the consultants are extremely helpful: American higher education has many competent, ethical, and valuable consultants. Some institutions that obtained Exxon grants regarded their consultants as crucial to their project's success. Nevertheless, several institutions reported truly miserable relationships with consultants. In Table 13 the first question shows how administrators viewed their consultants. The responses to this question indicate that the more successful projects had better relations with their consul-

Table 13. Percent of Administrators Agreeing with Evaluative Statements, by Categories of Colleges

			Category of College		
	Least Successful	Too Early to Tell	Successful Data-Bank MIS	Successful Advanced MIS	Successful MBO (with MIS)
1. Consultant services very helpful	14	26	20	22	30
2. Scope of the project too elaborate	13	5	17	0	12
3. Not enough training of local people	40	20	13	26	36
4. Lack of trained personnel on campus a problem	45	34	19	20	16
5. Presence of trained personnel on campus an advantage	28	10	23	35	28
6. Existing models/software a serious problem; did not meet needs; could not adjust	26	8	19	10	14
7. Existing models/software met needs	16	14	0	16	18
8. Previous data base constituted major problem	40	39	37	34	30
9. Project too complex for needs	22	13	10	1	7
10. Top administration fully supportive of project	53	80	88	83	87
11. Top administration heavily involved in project	24	12	50	41	73
12. Administrative turnover hurt project	22	12	0	17	3
13. Moderate or strong faculty support of project	13	71	34	36	76
14. Much turnover in project staffing	26	9	8	1	4
15. Not enough funding provided by Exxon	25	22	20	29	15

tants than the less successful ones.* Most notable is the fairly
low percentage of administrators in all institutions who said
that consultants' services were very helpful.

In our interviews we found the same pattern. A few people reported good relations, but many were very unhappy. One
insightful comment came from the president of a small college:
"Our consultants were not very helpful. Actually, I would say
that they were damn useless. In fact, I would even go further
than that: They were an absolute hindrance to our projects!
A slick group of guys who came in, sold us a bill of goods,
skipped town, and left us holding the bag. In the first place,
they oversold us. They insisted we needed stuff that we didn't
need at all. And after we bought all this expensive garbage, they
sent around their least experienced people to help. All in all, it
was a rotten experience. I guess they thought we were small college hicks out here in the boondocks, and they could get away
with murder, pulling the wool over our naive eyes."

Not everyone shared the feelings expressed by this president, but those feelings were sufficiently widespread to cause
grave concern. One trend was particularly apparent: most consulting firms had a vested interest in one type of project, and
they frequently pushed that approach even if it was not really
needed. One department chairman said: "The consultants came
around here and looked at our needs. Then, lo and behold,
they already had the answer in their little black bag! It seemed
to make absolutely no difference what our real needs were. The
solution in their bag was what they always prescribed." The tendency to push prepackaged products seemed to be a serious
shortcoming that undermined the effectiveness of the consulting firms. The lesson is obvious: The institution must assess its
own needs and look for consultants who can solve the problems.
It should not simply buy a consulting firm's bag of tricks.

There are risks and benefits to inside and outside talent.
The discussion about consultant shortcomings is not meant to
imply that consultants never play a valuable role. On the con-
trary, in many Exxon institutions they were helpful, provided

---

*A discussion of how projects were rated as more or less successful
is included in Chapter One.

valuable insights, and offered important technical skills. There is a constant debate over how much inside help outsiders can bring. There are certainly strengths and weaknesses in using an outside group, but there are also advantages and disadvantages to using inside talent. The question concerns appropriate balance.

The strengths of using an outside consultant lie in the fresh perspectives, the opportunity to obtain expertise where it is required, the insulation from internal politics that might color decisions, and the greater objectivity that comes from having no ego investment in the status quo. But there are also problems. One-shot consultants can fail to understand the dynamics of the unique local situation. "Objectivity" can be little more than ignorance. Outsiders can be used as "patsies" to support the policies of the chief administrator. In addition, channels for implementation are not open to an outside group, nor does a consultant have much ego investment (or authority) to *implement* recommendations. Finally, the outside consultant can be a scapegoat for either unhappy faculty members or unhappy administrators. Outsiders can be blamed for many sins after they are conveniently gone! (Is that part of the reason for the complaints we heard?)

Inside groups, such as a local task force, also have strengths and weaknesses. On the one hand, an inside group has insight that an outside team could never have. If composed of people with prestige and status within the institution, the home-front group will grant the project more legitimacy and help balance the charge that the consultants are administrative pawns. Most important, an internal task force has ego investment in implementing recommendations, not just filing and forgetting them. It constitutes a committed, interested party that can aid or challenge administrators during the implementation phase. On the other hand, an internal task force can create greater conflict. Political problems can be created within the college by recalling old battles and opening old wounds. It is important to articulate this negative feature. If such conflict does not occur at the planning stage, it will probably occur later. It is better to fight these battles head-on during the decision process, rather than underground later. Another disadvantage is additional cost in terms of money, commitment, and faculty and administrative time. Further, insiders may be so ego-involved and locked into old ways that they are unable to gain fresh perspectives on problems.

Obviously, the "insider versus outsider" argument is not easily settled. There are advantages and disadvantages to both styles of action. In many situations the most successful strategy is a combination in which outside consultants work with an internal task force. (For a more complete discussion of this issue see Baldridge and Deal, 1974, chap. 13.)

In the Exxon colleges, it appears that the most successful projects used outside consultants well, linking them with knowledgeable people within the institution. Often a task force of top-notch people was appointed to initiate the program and to work with consultants. In the less successful institutions, by contrast, it appeared that the consultants dropped in and dealt primarily with only one or two administrators. There seemed to be less internal support. Consequently, even competent consultants found themselves shackled because they did not have a strong link inside the institution.

The Early Stages: Political Aspects of Innovation

In *Power and Conflict in the University* Baldridge (1971) has discussed the political character of decision making in colleges and universities. We believe that the political dynamics are particularly important when management innovations, such as the RAMP projects, are introduced. Managerial innovations do not come into a vacuum. Every new program has to contend with the old programs for support, finances, and administrative attention. The administrators of old programs have a vested interest in protecting their domain. New programs almost always invade the traditional turf that other people have controlled in the past. It is no great surprise, then, that introducing a new program is a real political act. The old routines in traditional activities will quickly stomp out an innovation if it is not carefully protected. The project will die a quick death if the political dynamics are not carefully considered.

Is the college going to develop a new computer program to study faculty work load? If so, it should come as no great surprise that any faculty members who might show up poorly on that analysis will fight it tooth and nail. Is the college expecting to install a new planning officer to carry out a management by objectives program? No one should be shocked if the present assistant vice-president in charge of that function is less than helpful. Is the MIS project to spotlight the high expenses of the physics and chemistry departments? It is no wonder that those departments resist the program and claim that it produces "biased" data.

In short, new managerial techniques—like almost any other innovation—will inevitably step on toes, invade traditional domains, upset powerful people, and conflict with vested interests. For that reason, it is a delicate and complicated political task that requires homework and lining up necessary political support. It will be helpful to outline a few important characteristics of political processes in academic organizations.

First, almost all decisions are made by committees. In colleges and universities, there are many professional experts who claim—and usually get—the right to influence decisions. When the RAMP projects were beginning, the common pattern was to draw many experts together in a committee for decisions. The jokes about faculties establishing committees to make even the simplest decisions are true. But the committee structure is a natural outgrowth of academic organizations. Almost all major decisions made by administrators are somehow influenced by committee. The political tactics for dealing with committees are very important.

Second, there is a process of "fluid participation." Most people serving on committees are amateurs, engaging in their expert professions, not working full time as decision makers. They have many other things to do, and their attention span is limited. Consequently, they wander in and out of the decision process. Committees often have one group of people one week and another the next. One major problem in academic organizations is that committees are so haphazardly staffed. Power belongs to the people who stay long enough to exercise it. Those who want to influence decisions should concentrate their effort and stick with the process. People who stick to their guns usually win, while people who wander in and out find their influence limited. In several instances, people who technically were almost powerless gained significant influence on their campus RAMP project because they tenaciously worked on it while others gave it haphazard attention.

Third, there is an "issue carousel." Issues have a way of coming around again. Decisions are not made forever. Students, outsiders, faculty groups, and administrators push the same issues full circle time after time. Most of us have heard someone in a committee say, "But I remember when that exact same issue came up about a year ago, and we decided . . ." Many of the RAMP projects had historical roots in projects that previously were not funded but were resurrected when the Exxon funds became available.

Fourth, there is a "garbage can" process. The longer it takes to make a decision, the more complicated the issues become. People hope to accomplish several things at once, so they burden simple decisions with countless subsidiary topics. An issue that starts out simple will often wind up in a massive decision process resembling a Christmas tree, with hundreds of other issues tacked on. This is particularly true if the process is long and involved. We have all seen committees that started discussing a new student lounge but ended up proposing a whole new dormitory. And in the process the committee passed a resolution criticizing the trustees for their management of the capital improvement program! This "garbage can" process, common in colleges and universities, plagued many Exxon projects. The successful projects had administrators who knew how to "throw out the garbage," focus attention on the essentials, and get on with the project.

Fifth, conflict is common. Serious conflict occurs in any organization. But in colleges and universities, where it is fragmented into specialized subgroups with different interests, conflict becomes particularly fierce. On virtually every Exxon campus, there was evidence of conflict over the project. Some of it was minor; in other cases bitter feuds erupted. Conflict was probably a major problem for institutions that had expressed an interest in RAMP but had dropped it and never applied.

To summarize, academic decision processes are complex. They are not simple hierarchies like the processes in most business firms or government agencies. Administrators do not dominate the decision process. Instead, there is a complex process of decision by committee. Conflict is quite common among competing interest groups. Many processes occur: "fluid participation," with decision makers wandering in and out; an "issue carousel," with the same topics reappearing again and again; and a "garbage can" process, where issues get increasingly complicated as time goes on. Political counterthrusts will undermine managerial innovations unless we understand the political forces.

Some Rules for Effective Political Support

As we interviewed people on the Exxon campuses, we explored some of the political processes that occurred while the grants were being implemented. We observed a few tactics that seemed to work when political controversies arose, and we developed a few rules. It seems that the proponents of successful innovations had taken steps to help defuse the political situation. We will outline a few of these successful strategies.

Rule 1: Concentrate your efforts. People interested in changing the system frequently squander their efforts by chasing too many rainbows. An effective political change agent concentrates on only the important issues. Remember, most people do not care about most issues; they wander in and out. The person who sticks with one or two critical issues is most likely to win.

Rule 2: Know when to fight. A tactical genius knows which issue to choose. It makes sense to support issues when one can win. If it is obvious that you will lose, wait. Remember, with the "issue carousel," the situation will probably return, allowing time to muster resources for the next battle. There are, of course, exceptions to the "fight-to-win" rule. Sometimes it is wise to fight because the moral issue is great. Sometimes we can make future martyrs even if we lose now. The rule is usually to choose issues with high payoff. The sophisticated observer can usually tell the difference between a winner and a loser.

Rule 3: Learn the history. Every issue has roots deep in the past. The wise tactician searches for the historical bases of an issue. When was it around before? Who took which position? Who won? Who lost? The history can reveal which coalitions fight together and which tactics prove useful—information that helps in planning a strategy. The historically naive person is almost always a loser.

Rule 4: Build a coalition. Never go it alone. Good politicians know that much of their job involves building a political base to influence decisions. A dedicated cadre of change agents must be formed—a committed group of persons who exchange ideas and reinforce each other's efforts.

Rule 5: Join external constituencies. As we noted earlier, professional organizations usually have strong external constituents who apply pressure to the decision-making process. The wise strategist uses their support to influence the internal process. Insiders often naively overlook the political strategy of cultivating external allies. Welfare recipients and legislators can be strong forces in changing social welfare agencies; parents, alumni, and foundations can help change universities; community groups can be marshaled to transform public schools. The potential power of external constituencies must never be neglected.

Rule 6: Use committees wisely. Most major decisions in professional organizations are made by committees of experts who combine their specialized knowledge to solve problems. Therefore, organizational politics often centers around committee politics. Having influence on a committee is frequently equal to having influence over the decision.

How can one best use a committee to effect organizational change? First, get on the right committee by asking an appointment from an incumbent official. If the organization has a "committee on committees," this is a good place to start. Such rule-making appointive committees wield power in large professional organizations, and this power can be exploited to the best advantage.

Remember, "fluid participation" is a characteristic of professional organizations. The person who sticks with the committee is likely to have enormous impact. In a recent unpublished study, Steve Weiner of Stanford University analyzed decision making in a San Francisco school board committee charged with proposing plans for racial integration. He concluded that expertise, social prestige, and personality characteristics were important in the early stages of the committee's work. In later stages, however, those who persevered had the most influence. The first move, then, is to get on the committee, to be there regularly, and to stick it out even when others drop off.

The second rule for success on a committee is to do the homework. Expertise is vital in a professional organization. If one observes the earlier rule of concentrating efforts, there is more time to accumulate the knowledge to get ahead. Being chairman or secretary of a group is also useful. The chairman can set the agenda and call committee meetings, but the secretary controls the memory of the committee. Most members do not recall or care what is recorded in the minutes. By holding office, a committee member can reiterate the issues that he or she considers important—a definite advantage for political bargaining. Doing the homework—gathering knowledge, learning the history, being the chairman, or doing the secretarial chores—puts one in a strategically favorable position.

Finally, a major tactic on committees is to "fill the garbage can." Decision issues, like garbage cans, attract various irrelevant material. They can be used to the change agent's advantage. Dump new garbage into the can and then compromise readily on the unimportant issues. Loading the garbage can leaves plenty to bargain over when the deadlines are close. One can then insist stubbornly on retaining key issues.

Rule 7: Use the formal system. Colleges and universities have complex formal systems to carry out their activities. Naive change agents often are unaware that they can achieve a desired outcome simply by asking the appropriate official. This requires savvy and experience within the organization. Learn where the levers are and which ones to pull. Inexperienced change agents may fail to realize that most organizational officials are eager to please. Their success is difficult to judge because the tasks are often ambiguous. Consequently, most officials depend on "social validation" for judgments of success. That is, they are successful if people think they have done a good job. The ambiguity of the task, the lack of hard evaluation criteria, and the psychological need for approval among most administrators give partisans a tremendous advantage in getting things done. Do not forget a basic tactic: Ask for what you want!

Rule 8: Follow through to push the decision flow. We have said that the concept of "decision making" is a delusion. Decisions come unstuck, are reversed, get "unmade" during execution, or lose their impact as powerful political groups fight them. In real life, decisions go around in circles. The best one can hope for in the political battle is a temporary win. The aware politician knows that he must keep an eye on important decisions even after they have supposedly been made. What happens after the committee has reached its decision? Often, the decision evaporates! The person who traces the decision flow through to execution, and fights when issues are distorted, is the one who really has the power. The partisan who is dedicated to change will be a tenacious watchdog. He will monitor the steps of the decision, staying on administrators' backs and calling public attention to administrative lapses.

There are a few tricks to following through. First, be sure to get deadlines on decisions. Delay is the enemy of change; deadlines are flags that call attention to stalling. Second, give the idea a sheltered start. If placed back into the regular routine of the organization, a change will usually be smothered by powerful old routines. The shrewd planner shelters the change in its infancy, which often means giving the program a home under the wing of a strong, hospitable executive. Only after the new idea has established roots should it be placed in the organization's regular structure.

Several followthrough techniques involve people. Have allies in the vanguard of change. If people embodying your ideas are running the show, the change is likely to succeed. In addition, the reward system is important. If you want things to change, reward change-promoting behavior. If a straightforward award (such as money) is inappropriate, prestige and public acclaim can be equally valuable.

Political Dynamics in the RAMP Projects

The Heavy-Handed President. One of the most fascinating political dynamics to emerge from our interviews was the case of one heavy-handed administrator in a small liberal arts college. By almost universal agreement, the president ran a tight ship. The Higher Education Research Institute team surveyed the faculty at the beginning of the project. The questionnaires showed that the vast majority gave the college an extremely low rating on democratic governance. Faculty members felt that the president was a "strong" leader and that the faculty had little influence on decision making.

The president became quite interested in new managerial techniques. He helped write the proposal for an Exxon RAMP grant. One administrator discussed with us how that grant was originally viewed: "It is clear that our Exxon grant was viewed with outright hostility by most faculty. Frankly, most of us assumed it would be a tool for the president to get information and use it against us. The whole project was seen as a ploy to fence us in even more than before. It is no secret around here that the grant met a chilly reception among faculty and department heads."

After this initial hostility toward the project and the president, a curious thing happened. The president, who was pushing the project hard, had involved many people in it. Several influential faculty members decided that if they couldn't beat the president at his own game, they would try to co-opt the project and use it against him. So this group organized an informal coalition and began to participate regularly in the project workshops and planning sessions. They came to all the meetings, concentrated their efforts, and deliberately took control of the committees that ran the program. The unwary president enthusiastically embraced the new group and their commitment to "his" project.

Within a year this determined group had wrested control of the project from the president. What had been viewed as the president's tool to control the faculty was now in the hands of that faculty. The chairman of one of the largest departments told us the following: "To the president's great surprise, he woke up one morning and found the Exxon program had severely undermined his arbitrary power. Those of us who had engineered the transition were actually about as shocked as he was. We found that he reluctantly shared budget information with us, and that many of the decisions that he had made out of his coat pocket were now subject to public discussion. He does deserve credit, however, for when he saw the direction the project was taking, he embraced it fully. I think he really changed many of his practices. Everyone was rather surprised—including him, I'm sure! He certainly didn't start out as a 'democratic' leader. But the project's force, the public discussions occurring with it, and his commitment to linking the budget to those public planning sessions caused a fairly dramatic shift in his position. The cat had been encircled by the mice and it was his own mousetrap that did it!"

This case was probably the most colorful example of RAMP politics. Everyone we talked to in that institution discussed the political dynamics more than the technical characteristics of the project. Our interviews consistently showed that people believed the president's administrative style had changed strikingly—that the college's government was more democratic— at the project's close. In short, the political dynamics accompanying the RAMP grant brought significant changes.

Dean of Students Versus Academic Dean. Another interesting political case occurred at a large private liberal arts college. We found that, during the planning stages for the RAMP grant, a major fight had occurred between the dean of students and the academic dean. Everyone agreed that the objective of the RAMP project would be to set up a sophisticated management information system and design computer programs that would produce information for decision making. A dispute arose, however, over *which information* would go into the system. The academic dean insisted that the principal components should be faculty and staffing patterns and financial issues. He wanted to deal primarily with budget questions and faculty positions in various departments. Thus, he made a forceful argument to limit the system to those items. The dean of students argued that the MIS should also collect significant data about students and their progress. The dean wanted information about student satisfaction with counseling and guidance, academic advising, and the quality of residence-hall life. He also felt that it would be a major educational breakthrough to record standardized test scores on students in the data bank. In this way, the actual learning achievement of students could be linked to the staffing patterns in various departments. In short, the dean of students was proposing a radical idea: that information on *students' progress* and *educational outcomes* be introduced into the system. He argued that merely gathering data on finances and staffing would limit the program to the bureaucratic processes. Educational outcome would not be tapped.

The fight over this issue started slowly. In one large planning session, the dean of students presented his idea, which was received warmly. Many were enthusiastic that actual educational outcomes, as well as financing and staffing issues, would be part of the data base. In fact, one faculty member at that meeting told us the following: "The initial reaction to the dean of students' proposal was genuine excitement. People discussed how the educational process would be influenced if we all had some information about student satisfaction and academic progress in our programs. In fact, during that meeting it was clear that the dean of students was swaying the committee away from the academic dean's stress on funding and staffing."

Then, suddenly, between that meeting and the next, the political currents shifted. At the next meeting there was outraged opposition to the dean of students' position. It seemed that, as people began to think about the issue, they realized how dangerous data on student outcomes could be. What if such data showed that anthropology students did poorly compared with sociology students? What if student satisfaction in the social sciences was much higher than in the hard sciences? What if students consistently complained of poor academic advising in the humanities? Who would know this? What action would be taken? One administrator commented on the change in mood: "At this meeting the dean of students was on the defensive. The initial support had been completely undermined. I don't know if the academic dean talked to people privately, but by this meeting most of the faculty had made a 180-degree turn. They were absolutely opposed to the dean of students' idea. It was just too politically hot to handle. People were embarrassed to say so, but they feared that student feedback about their teaching and departmental activities would be painful. They began to see the fairly neutral staffing and budgeting stuff as much less threatening. The pendulum now smashed back in favor of the academic dean's 'safer' proposal. This meeting was the death knell for the dean of students' idea. He left hot and angry and never came back to any subsequent meetings. Shortly thereafter we submitted an Exxon proposal which didn't even mention student-based data. The politics of the situation had shifted dramatically."

At nearly all the Exxon institutions, we continually ran across political fights that determined the shape of the project. Programs that looked matter of fact and almost "scientific" on paper really had a deep, tangled background of academic politics. We learned from our interviews that the introduction of a new management procedure is an eminently political enterprise.

Introducing the Project

Let us assume that the political battles have been won, and the project has matured into a new phase. It has been initiated into the system, and there are many factors likely to undermine success. We will examine some rules for introducing the project.

Don't promise the moon. Promising the moon is one of the most successful strategies—if you want the project to fail! Consider this situation: A small liberal arts college obtains a substantial Exxon grant for a management information system. A high-powered consultant from an outside firm arrives, preaching the gospel about how the firm plans to save the institution. A director is appointed. Immediately, his ego is wrapped up in the project. He joins the chorus singing praises of the project.

Interest in the activity is high. Unfortunately, this scenario is common. At this early stage, expectations rise and hopes wax strong. Later in the game, almost everyone will realize that the promises were too grand and that the fevered pitch should have been tempered. This evangelistic style will lead to deflated egos and unfulfilled expectations.

Keep a sensible profile. This is more on the same theme. Our research team was at a small college when the new project director was introduced at a faculty assembly. The president stood up; discussed the new Exxon grant in glowing terms; and introduced the director, who informed the assembly that the project would transform the college's entire decision-making process. The faculty could not help but expect this project to solve all its problems. Two years later, during our site visit, almost everyone expressed a sense of failure—of being cheated out of results promised glowingly at that assembly. A lower profile, more realistic expectations, and less optimism from the director would probably have resulted in a more favorable evaluation of the project's success.

Keep the scope of the project in bounds. Grandiose promises are made because the administration and the program director actually believe that the project will make a great difference. In fact, the scope of the project was usually out of proportion to the modest money offered in the Exxon program. Unfortunately, in trying to convince a foundation that funds are needed, a college tends to promise too much. Throughout some of the original grant proposals were scattered such phrases as "changing the entire decision-making structure," "revitalizing the administrative process," and "meeting the financial crisis head-on." In light of these extravagant claims, it is not surprising that some considered the project's scope entirely too large (see Table 13, Question 2).

Staff the program with competent personnel. It was amazing how many Exxon projects had trouble recruiting and maintaining a first-class staff. In Table 13 Questions 3, 4, and 5 show how significant the staffing problem was. Fully 45 percent of the administrators in the colleges with unsuccessful projects regarded the lack of trained personnel as a serious problem. In the more successful projects, the percentages fell dramatically. A substantial minority of administrators felt that there was not enough training of local people. Some 40 percent of the administrators in the least successful institutions complained about the lack of training.

It seems that the absence of qualified specialists and the lack of long-term training were serious barriers to implementation. Of course, most of the Exxon institutions were small liberal arts colleges that were unlikely to have people with extensive managerial training and computer skills on their staffs. Still, it is surprising that these people did not attain those skills once the projects were started. In our interviews we got the distinct impression that some administrators were quite naive about the skills needed to implement the program successfully.

Too often the project staff directors were assigned duties without enough attention to whether they had the necessary skills. The pattern was typical: a middle-level administrator loaded with responsibilities simply had the project activities tacked on; frequently, he did not even possess the critical skills. Many of these small colleges could not afford to hire additional staff, knowing that they might have to discharge them once the grant ran out. Nevertheless, it seems that something could have been done to obtain the necessary talent and manpower.

Another typical pattern was to staff the program with a person whose skills were extremely narrow and technical. The director of the computer center would often be placed in charge of a management information system. Then, following his natural inclination, he would overwhelm everybody with the system's technical characteristics. The more general administrators would withdraw because they felt overwhelmed with technical details. Although this type of director is very skilled, he is so specialized that the general administrative staff do not interact well with him. Hiring people without needed skills is self-defeating, but hiring a narrow technocrat also can undermine the project.

Political neutrality is another qualification for a director. The project head needs the confidence and support of a broad spectrum of the campus community. In particular, he or she should not be deeply entangled in local campus politics. The di-

managerial data to make decisions. But none of them ever talked to me. It was clear that they would pay no attention to the information I gave them. Maybe I did something to offend them. Maybe they felt threatened. I don't know what it was, but the bottom line was that there was no support whatsoever. That indifference is what killed the project. I finally got fed up with nobody listening and resigned. Nothing else has been done since with the project."

A third project director illustrated the importance of *continual* administrative support. "This project was the brain child of the academic vice-president. The president didn't know much about it but was fully supportive. However, disaster struck when the academic vice-president left. The project was set adrift. In fact, the new man that came in was determined to destroy this leftover vestige of his predecessor's reign. He was out to get me and this project from day one. At first the president made noises about standing behind me. But after awhile he made peace with the new vice-president at our expense. The turnover changed us overnight from the guys that could do no wrong to the guys that could do no right. There was nothing traumatic about the project's death. It just gradually ceased to exist because nobody cared."

So we see that these projects, even after getting off to a good start, cannot be abandoned if they are to be successful. They require continual nurturance.

Faculty support is also critical. Although most of the RAMP projects were more influenced by administrative behavior, they seemed to flourish more with faculty support. This is particularly true of the management by objectives programs (see Table 13). Question 13 shows that 76 percent of respondents in the successful projects with management by objectives systems had strong faculty support. This contrasts sharply with the 13 percent who report faculty support in the less successful schools. The 71 percent reporting faculty support in the "too early to tell" category is easily interpreted. Most recent RAMP grants were given for management by objectives programs. In these programs, faculty involvement and participation is a major objective, whereas the MIS programs deal primarily with administrative data. So faculty support is especially critical to MBO projects. That added measure of support, however, will give a boost to any type of program.

The project needs a security blanket. New programs are completely vulnerable. Much attention must be given to their structural and administrative location within the college. If a managerial innovation is attached to an ongoing program in the middle ranks of the bureaucracy, it usually washes out quickly. One of the most common mistakes we observed was to propose a planning process that affected top administrators and then locate the program in the computer center. Immediately, the program was tagged as a technical matter and a middle-level administrative concern. The top administrators did not view it as part of their domain. And the computer center director often viewed it as an unimportant stepchild foisted on him in addition to his other activities. By contrast, the programs that worked directly out of the office of a president or an academic vice-president were much more visible and had greater interaction with top administration. In addition, when it was under the protection of a powerful administrator, the project was sheltered from attack by traditional administrators who felt threatened.

Staff turnover kills a project. A most important factor in a successful project is continuity in a well-trained staff. We found that projects were severely undermined when key staff members left. Since small liberal arts colleges might have only one or two people with the technical skills for the project, the project often collapsed when a key person left. Internal transfers were also frequent. We suspected that some small colleges were using their local "troubleshooters" for the projects. A highly competent person might be moved around like a chessman from position to position. While this allowed a number of brush fires to be fought with one person, it undermined the strength of any given project.

The problem of staff turnover shows up vividly in Table 13, Question 14. In most institutions this problem is negligible. Nevertheless, of the institutions that were least successful, fully one fourth complained of having staff turnover. This figure is six or eight times higher than that in the more successful institutions. An interview at one small religious college illustrates the problem dramatically: "We started our Exxon project because a bright young administrator wanted to experiment with a management information system. He was quite an expert in the area, having worked with business organizations on the same problem. He convinced the president that this was a good idea and attended several workshops which taught him how to use the programs. Well, we got an MIS. No sooner did it get under way than talented Mr. X with his newly acquired skills found a better job at another institution. He left with less than a month's notice. Now we are left with a file cabinet full of junk, a computer software program that nobody knows how to use, and printouts that routinely come to administrators with absolutely no meaning to anybody. Our project is dead as a doornail because we lost a key fellow."

Financial starvation is a quick way to kill a project. In our research on the RAMP projects, we found that projects with severe funding difficulties often collapsed, while the institutions that had made substantial contributions along with the Exxon grant had the most success. Of course, the Exxon proposals all required some matching funds. Some institutions took this seriously, however, and others did not. The "on-paper" version of the institution's contribution can look very promising while the funds are actually quite slim. Matching funds are particularly critical for the continuity of the project. In those institutions making major contributions, the projects stayed healthy long after the Exxon funding expired. By contrast, projects that depended largely on Exxon money withered when the funds dried up. Clearly, if the institution cares enough about the project to contribute substantially, the chances for success are much higher.

Planning for the Death of the Project

Projects like those funded by the Exxon grants must eventually die. That death will probably occur in one of three ways. The project may die from a burnout of interest and enthusiasm. Management innovation projects are like many love affairs: Early excitement turns to later boredom. Many projects die as interest wanes and people go on to new activities. When the initial staff move on, the new staff may not have the interest or missionary zeal that surrounded the project at birth. Between 20 percent and 35 percent of the Exxon projects (depending on who was judging and how) died because enthusiasm diminished, funding was cut, or key staff people moved on.

A second pattern is the spawning of new children. As the original project faded into the background, new activities were often spawned. The RAMP grants stirred up the initial enthusiasm and got the program started; after the money ran out, other grants were secured from other foundations, Title III, or other federal agencies. In fact, our interviews with project directors suggest that 41 percent of all the RAMP projects eventually led to another grant in the same general area of management improvement. Another 22 percent were "planning" to apply for such grants at the time of our interviews. Following are some examples of offspring from Exxon RAMP grants.

1. One college became involved in a faculty development model. The Exxon project gave the institution the needed confidence, and it subsequently got a grant from the Lilly Endowment.
2. One college initiated a long-range financial-planning project. Its need was identified through RAMP. It became involved with NCHEMS, funded by the Northwest Area Foundation.
3. One college obtained a grant from the Kellogg Foundation for a faculty development and academic-planning program, using RAMP methods.
4. Another college obtained several grants for projects that spun off from RAMP. The college obtained money from the National Science Foundation for some planning in the natural sciences. It received a grant to study new instructional methods and their effect on productivity, and a grant to study the college's accounting system, which has facilitated a 30 percent turnaround in the cash-flow problem.

A third pattern is institutionalization of the project, in which the project becomes an ongoing part of the routine administration. This kind of "death" is really only a loss of identity and probably the most typical pattern. In fact, it is the pattern that the Exxon Foundation explicitly desired. As the project matures, it simply becomes less visible. If they are really successful, the planning and data gathering become part of the standard operating procedure. The staff become just another staff among many.

Max Weber once noted that social movements, such as political parties, move from "charismatic" leaders to "bureaucratic" leaders. In a sense, these management projects do the same. Early directors are movers and shakers, planners and activists. Later, however, activities become more routine and bureaucratic; the leadership of the project shifts to a solid administrator. The life cycle of the project comes full circle: from routine operation before the project is started, through the excited activity of the early stages of the project, and finally back to the routine system as the project gains a place in the normal process.

Chapter Nine

Controlling
College Costs

During our research on the campuses, we were usually trying to determine the direct impact of MIS and MBO. But on numerous occasions campus leaders talked to us about general financial issues and shared with us their successes—and sometimes their failures—in keeping finances under control. It was useful to look over the shoulders of these institutional leaders at steps they are taking to handle the cost-income squeeze. There are no brilliant theoretical insights here, no panaceas to save colleges, no blueprints that promise salvation. Since similar activities are taking place on most campuses, most of what we are reporting will sound familiar. However, sharing ideas about "how other folks handle the problem" might be useful. The discussion is divided into two parts: institutional efforts to *increase income* and to *reduce costs*.

Strategies to Increase Income

Table 14 describes the distribution of current fund revenues for the twenty-eight RAMP institutions that provided financial data. (Some of the institutions with MBO systems did not furnish financial data, since their projects did not focus on financial matters.) The percentages indicate that these institutions depend on tuition and fees for approximately two thirds of their revenues—about the same percentage as other institutions in three recent surveys of the financial condition of private higher education (Bowen and Minter, 1975, 1976; Minter and Bowen, 1977). Government appropriations constitute the fastest-growing source of revenues for these colleges, up from 7.7 percent in 1972 to 9.6 percent in 1976. The second fastest-growing source of revenue is gifts. However, colleges have been experiencing a reduction in gifts since 1973–74, probably because of the recession. Reliance on voluntary support has always been viewed by institutions with ambivalence. On the one hand, an increase in gift income slows the rate of increase in student tuition and fees and, in the face of increasing competition with the public sector, benefits the institution. On the other hand, voluntary support is unstable, as demonstrated during the recent recession. Further, the use of private gifts in *current* operations may reduce the support of various philanthropic groups for *capital* campaigns. Donors usually like to leave something tangible behind, such as a building; they are usually not happy if their gifts disappear in payments on the monthly fuel bill. In the long run, a policy of using gifts to pay current bills may lead to an overall deterioration in the physical plant.

New Sources of Income

Liberal arts colleges have traditionally responded to financial problems by attempting to develop new revenue sources. For instance, these institutions have turned increasingly to the federal government for assistance. However, with a vast array of social programs competing with postsecondary education for the federal dollar, it seems unlikely that federal largess will be a source of many new funds. Thus, for the immediate future at least, funds beyond the current $12 billion will probably not be allocated to postsecondary education. Most federal programs are designed to eliminate financial barriers to equal educational opportunity; they are designed to make grants to students, not to

Table 14. Revenues: Distribution of Current Fund Income for Selected Purposes

		Percentage Distribution			Average Annual Compound Growth Rate, 1972–73 to 1975–76
	1972–73	1973–74	1974–75	1975–76	
I. Educational and general revenues	76.6	78.0	78.3	78.7	7.7
Where Does the Money in I. Come From?					
Tuition revenues	67.1	63.4	65.0	65.0	7.5
Government appropriations	7.7	8.3	8.6	9.6	15.0
Gift income	11.1	14.7	13.6	12.7	9.5
Endowment income	5.4	6.7	6.3	5.5	5.6
Other	8.7	6.9	6.5	7.2	–
II. Auxiliary enterprises	23.4	22.0	21.7	21.3	-4.0
III. Total revenues	100.0	100.0	100.0	100.0	7.0

Note: N = 28 Exxon institutions.

institutions. It is improbable that resources will be shifted from the current financial aid programs to direct aid for institutions.

A second source of financial assistance is the various state governments. One argument for state support of private institutions is that lower state expenditures are required than if the same students were at public institutions. However, the current demographic trend suggests that these additional state expenditures will be harder to get as public institutions scramble to maintain their current enrollment levels. Further, any state assistance is likely to be attached to control by the state coordinating board. Many private institutions see this as a threat to their autonomy. Whether the financial pressures will be sufficient to drive private institutions into agreements with state coordinating boards remains to be seen.

The decline in size of the traditional college cohort leads to a third possible source of new revenues: nontraditional students. The development of this new market is supported by three current trends: the rationale of lifelong learning, the decline in the length of the average workweek, and the expansion of employee educational benefits. For instance, General Motors has tuition-remission benefits amounting to $900 for each of its 700,000 employees. If fully utilized, this would amount to the staggering sum of over $600 million in educational benefits. However, to develop this market fully, colleges must offer programs in which nontraditional students may enroll, and offer them in convenient geographical areas.

Two examples of the development of these new markets by the RAMP institutions follow. The College of St. Thomas in Minneapolis recently instituted a graduate program leading to a master's degree in business administration, with courses offered at times convenient to persons who are fully employed. The introduction of this degree followed the college's assessment of the potential market in the greater Minneapolis–St. Paul area. The program, a problem-oriented approach to studying management, differs from the MBA program offered at the University of Minnesota, which has dominated the area. A second program designed to attract the nontraditional college student was instituted by Adelphi University on Long Island. This program in business administration is known as EDUTRAIN. This program goes to the students; courses are offered on the commuter train between Long Island and New York City. In this way people can earn an MBA degree while commuting. The Adelphi program has not only been a source of revenues; it has also provided the university with a great deal of favorable public relations.

While it is possible for a college, with sufficient planning and analysis, to identify potential new markets of nontraditional students, the development of this source is not a panacea for liberal arts colleges. For instance, only 7,000 of 700,000 employees have participated in the General Motors tuition-remission program. Perhaps a large unmet demand does not really exist for postsecondary education among nontraditional students. It takes approximately five part-time students to equal one full-time-equivalent (FTE) student. The fundamental question is whether there are sufficient numbers of nontraditional students available to an institution to offset the decline in the traditional cohort.

More Effective Admissions Activities

One administrator at West Virginia Wesleyan University observed that the enrollment decline in traditional students caused him to sleep like a baby: he would wake up and cry every hour! West Virginia Wesleyan faced a precipitous decline in enrollment in the early 1970s. The president at that time, John D. Rockefeller, decided to allocate more resources to the admissions office, since 80 percent of the institution's revenues were derived from student tuition and fees. The additional staff and resources, plus personal letters to admittants and special admissions programs, turned the enrollment situation around.

Many colleges have taken steps to monitor their admissions efforts. Colleges must carefully consider their enrollment goals, projecting a modest increase. With a goal for the admissions office established, it is possible to generate a number of performance measures. The first is the ratio of "applications" to "initial contacts." Meeth (1974) has suggested that this ratio constitutes an important area for examination because it shows how effective the college's presentation is. A second measure is the ratio of "matriculants" to "admittants." Possibly, however, this ratio is controlled more by the availability of financial aid than by traditional admissions practices.

Such performance measures must be further categorized by type of student or by the geographical area from which the student applied. Many institutions have become increasingly concerned about their mix of students. For example, many private colleges are concerned that enrollment distribution is becoming "wasp-waisted," heavy on rich students who can pay their way and disadvantaged students who receive aid, but light on middle-class students who have neither the wealth nor the financial aid. By monitoring the admissions of new students by their characteristics, colleges will be better able to move toward the student-mix goals of the college. Alternatively, institutions also can separate their admissions performance measures according to the geographical regions that traditionally have supplied students. Sectarian institutions (such as Gustavus Adolphus College and Oklahoma Baptist University) have traditionally drawn students from certain congregations. By separating performance measures by geographical areas and by various congregational student pools, the colleges can assess the effectiveness of various recruitment strategies.

To implement procedures such as these institutions obviously must have relatively sophisticated information systems. Such systems constantly monitor various performance measures to identify possible problem areas (such as lower ratio of "contracts" to "applicants") in a given geographical area or in a certain group of high schools. Once a possible problem has been identified, such systems help explain the problem and suggest corrective action. A number of RAMP institutions had longitudinal admissions files; Pacific Union College had an on-line admissions-processing capability since the early 1970s.

The development of incentive systems for admissions officers and staff is also possible for closer scrutiny of the program. Performance measures can serve as the foundation of personnel evaluation, the distribution of financial rewards, and decisions on promotion and termination. Under such incentive plans, admissions offices become less a center for processing applications and more a "marketing" division. Combined with the entry of commercial marketing organizations in student recruitment programs, such incentive programs may result in increasingly sophisticated admissions operations.

More Effective Development Programs

Another major revenue-generating unit in a private college is the development office. Gifts and grants are relatively unstable. If gift income is less than anticipated, a budget deficit may occur. As noted earlier, Furman University instituted a "deferred gift income plan." This method of accounting allowed the institution to spend gift income obtained in one year in the subsequent budget period, thus evening out the flow of gift income and making the budget more predictable.

Like the admissions programs, the development program can be monitored with a variety of performance measures. One is the ratio of total revenues generated to dollars spent to obtain them. This measure assesses the effectiveness of alternative strategies to increase voluntary support. Incentive structures for the staff of development offices can be developed. The same considerations are involved here as with the management of college admissions offices.

Performance measures can also be used to assess the effectiveness of alternative strategies in major fund-raising campaigns. For instance, Furman decided to employ a number of professional development staff members to maintain a relatively low-level but constant fund-raising campaign. This strategy differs substantially from the traditional liberal arts development approach of retaining an outside consultant. Assessing this strategy would be impossible without some performance measure.

The assessment of alternative programs is somewhat complex for a development office. Typically, development offices in private colleges are responsible not only for fund raising but also for relations with alumni and other support groups. One alternative is to consider that both missions have the generation of revenues as the ultimate outcome—at least for cost-accounting purposes. In this case, expenditures on alumni publications and similar activities are combined with those for various fund-raising efforts to provide one overall level of expenditures. The ratio of total gifts generated (for current and plant funds) to expenditures used collecting these funds would provide the measure of performance. A second possible approach is to assess each mission independently. In this case, expenditures for alumni publications and communications-related activities are separated from those directly related to the fund-raising efforts. Such an approach would obviously result in a different measure of performance.

Which measure should be used? Alternative measures of performance provide different incentives to the person doing the job, and they are likely to affect the outcome. For example, to exclude alumni publications expenditures from the development office's performance measure is likely to result in a deemphasis on them. In the long run, this may have a detrimental effect on the institution's ability to generate voluntary support from its various constituencies. However, to *include* these communications-related expenditures in a measure of performance is likely to overstate the costs of raising money from gifts. There is no "correct" way to formulate a performance measure. But people's behavior will definitely be affected differently by alternative strategies, and setting the criteria calls for careful thought about the consequences.

Strategies to Reduce Costs

Up to this point, we have discussed strategies used by various RAMP colleges to increase *revenues*; let us now look at the expenditure side of the coin. The fundamental fact of life for colleges is that costs will continue to increase. Policies that significantly affect costs may be changed, but such changes have only a short-term effect. For instance, it is possible to change the student/faculty ratio, as many RAMP institutions did. This change will affect the basis on which costs increase, but it will not halt the rate of increase. Thus, colleges are constantly faced with achieving a balance between cost and revenue increases.

The pattern of expenditures for the "average" RAMP institution is presented in Table 15. These data indicate that slightly over 40 percent of an institution's educational and general expenditures go to instruction (taken as a percentage of *total* expenditures, this percentage would be reduced to 30 percent).

Table 15. Expenditures: Distribution of Current Funds for Selected Purposes

	Percentage Distribution				Average Annual Compound Growth Rate, 1972–73 to 1975–76
	1972–73	1973–74	1974–75	1975–76	
I. Educational and general expenditures	70.4	70.5	70.6	70.2	6.3
Where Is the Money in I. Spent?					
Instructional expenditures	43.4	44.2	43.6	42.7	6.1
Sponsored research	6.9	7.3	7.4	7.5	6.6
Student services	7.8	7.8	7.9	8.0	7.2
Plant maintenance	10.8	10.7	10.5	10.9	10.1
Other	31.1	30.0	30.6	30.9	5.8
II. Student aid	8.2	8.9	9.4	10.0	12.6
III. Auxiliary enterprises	21.4	20.6	20.0	19.8	5.1
IV. Total expenditures	100.0	100.0	100.0	100.0	6.4

Note: N = 28 Exxon institutions.

This category is composed of all expenditures for faculty salaries, supplies, and equipment for the various academic departments. It is surprising, especially for these teaching-oriented campuses, to find that less than half of the funds designated for educational purposes is spent on these activities.

Today's pattern of expenditures, displayed in Table 15, differs from that of earlier years. In the past, expenditures for "instruction and departmental research" have been relatively constant; they constituted roughly half of an institution's educational and general expenditures (National Federation of College and University Business Officers Associations, 1960; Jenny and Wynn, 1970). Since the beginning of this decade, there has been a gradual decrease, so that now slightly over 40 percent of the expenditures go for instruction and research. The "other" category under educational and general expenditures consists of academic support activities, such as the library, and general administrative services. As Table 15 indicates, almost one third of the average institution's educational expenditures is consumed by this category.

Student aid expenditures account for a little less than 10 percent of an institution's total expenditures, and a substantial proportion of this money comes from outside the institution—from the Basic Educational Opportunity Grants, for example. Jenny and Wynn (1970), however, noted that there is a growing gap between the revenues earmarked for student aid and total institutional expenditures for student aid. Institutions have been forced to provide institutional resources to fill the gap. They realize the necessity to spend money to get and keep their students, but the price is a constant drain on resources.

A comparison of Tables 14 and 15 underlines the fundamental financial problem facing private liberal arts colleges—balancing income and outgo. Until today at least, colleges have managed to keep an unsteady balance between total revenues and expenditures—primarily by drastically curtailing the rate of growth in expenditures, rather than increasing income. Specifically, one technique has been to slow the increase in faculty salaries. The unresolved question is whether private colleges will be able to retain this relative balance in the face of declining enrollments.

Instructional Expenditures. Because higher education is a labor-intensive industry, one prime way to control expenditures is to manipulate faculty compensation or size. Generally, institutions have employed four strategies.

First, *faculty salary increases have diminished.* For example, Wesleyan had generally averaged about 7 percent per year for salary increases until the mid 1970s. The university estimated that each 1 percent increase in salaries resulted in a total increase in expenditures of $100,000 per year. Further, there is a cumulative effect to faculty salary increases: an increase in one year serves as the base rate for future increases. Consequently, Wesleyan, like many other institutions, tried to reduce the growth rate. The goal was to hold increases to 4 percent per year.

Second, colleges have *reduced the number of faculty.* This reduction has usually been accomplished through "orderly attrition." As indicated in Chapter Three, Wesleyan decided to reduce the size of the faculty by forty positions by not filling vacancies as they occurred. The net effect was to increase the student/faculty ratio. In other cases, however, the reduction in faculty has coincided with declining student enrollments. These institutions, like Alice in Wonderland, "ran harder and harder, just to stand still." Despite staff reductions, the cost per student has still increased. The decline in enrollments has exceeded the institution's ability to reduce faculty. This trend is one of the most dismal harbingers of things to come for higher education.

Third, colleges have adopted policies of *replacing senior faculty who leave with junior faculty.* For instance, the biology department at Clarkson College decided to replace a full professor retiring in 1973 with an assistant professor. The cost saving to the department was, in 1976, $7,632 (or $47 per FTE student). In the future, the recruitment of most new faculty probably will come at the assistant professor level to effect savings and to acquire talent fresh from graduate school for increasingly "tenured-up" departments. Some institutions have also begun to retain more part-time faculty. This policy provides flexibility in allocating faculty to departments experiencing enrollment increases.

Another policy change that has impact on instructional costs is *changing the student/faculty ratio*. Several RAMP institutions decided to change the ratio by a combined policy of increasing the number of students and reducing the faculty through attrition. An alternative strategy, used by Carroll College in Wisconsin, was to increase faculty work loads, requiring members to teach more hours per year. As Bowen and Douglas (1971) have indicated, the increase in the total faculty work load is one potential source of reducing cost. The long-term effect of such a change is roughly equivalent to an increase in the student/faculty ratio.

To summarize, the RAMP institutions frequently used four strategies to reduce costs: reducing salaries, cutting back faculty, replacing senior with junior faculty, and increasing student/faculty ratios. By mentioning these strategies, we do not intend to *endorse* them as attractive options. In fact, it seems fair to say that all these strategies erode academic quality. Cutting salaries can decrease the attractiveness of any institution. More critically, decreased salaries can drive quality people out of academe and into other careers—an outcome many shortsighted administrators have missed as they smugly believed the job shortage in academe would allow them to treat faculty poorly. Replacing senior people with junior appointments will eventually hurt also. In short, each of these strategies may save money, but the price is high. The erosion of quality may be inevitable, but certainly not a trend to be embraced lightly.

In the long run, the fundamental problem facing the liberal arts college is developing an attractive academic program. Increasingly, the liberal arts college faces a serious dilemma, one characterized by the "balloon analogy" used by a department chairperson at Otterbein College: "The instructional program is like the ballast in a balloon on a flight over the Atlantic Ocean. The balloon is losing air and rapidly falling toward the icy ocean. The balloonist is frantically discarding ballast, hoping he will be able to remain airborne long enough to reach the mainland. We're doing the same—throwing out programs, cutting positions, hiring part-timers, anything to keep afloat. We aren't certain the mainland is really there. We may throw away our ballast, but still sink."

The college administrator is faced with a terrible dilemma. There is constant financial pressure to reduce programs in academic departments with declining enrollments. But those reductions may reduce the attractiveness of that program for students and lead, in turn, to further enrollment reductions. It is a vicious circle. Consequently, it is increasingly important for colleges to do "forward" programming in which a specific student clientele is identified and a specific program designed. The college must be willing to risk the resources necessary to start a program to attract that clientele.

Administrative Expenditures. As Table 15 indicates, roughly 50 percent of educational and general expenditures go for activities other than direct teaching and research. Most computer-based MIS networks are primarily designated to control instructional costs. These institutions also have employed a wide range of alternatives to deal with burgeoning administrative expenditures.

Wesleyan University began one of the most aggressive efforts to reduce administrative expenditures. The university was attempting to reduce its spending by at least 10 percent. As with instructional expenditures, any reduction in general administrative services primarily involves reducing personnel or their compensation. The progress at Wesleyan was impressive, even though it was not entirely successful in the face of rapid inflation.

A second area of concern deals with student services. As indicated earlier, expenditures for student administrative services are one of the fastest-growing elements in an institution's cost structure. The RAMP institutions have taken several steps to control these expenditures. For instance, Wesleyan University attempted to reorganize its various student service offices in the hope of reducing the number of staff—particularly secretarial-clerical. In addition, it reduced the number of head residents in each dormitory by one and the level of compensation for both head residents and resident advisers. As another example, the

College of Saint Thomas considered contracting out its dormitory operations to a commercial organization. One wonders why profit-oriented commercial organizations are able to provide this service cheaper than the college can.

A third area of administrative services involves maintenance of the physical plant. Deferring plant maintenance has obviously been a way to reduce growth in expenditures. Not only have needed repairs been delayed, but the number of maintenance positions has been reduced. For instance, Wesleyan University proposed to eliminate certain carpentry and mechanical positions and to increase student employment. The reason is obvious: Wesleyan pays for the regular employees, but 80 percent of the cost for student personnel is paid by the federal government. As another example, Illinois Wesleyan University purchased a computer to control the use of energy. According to university personnel, cost savings from reduced energy consumption more than offset the computer's purchase price within one year.

One final area of nonacademic expenditures involves financial aid. This area poses a difficult problem for private liberal arts colleges. On the one hand, most institutions realize that they must spend money to attract students. Student aid is particularly important for private institutions, where the high tuition costs are partly offset by student aid. On the other hand, as Jenny and Wynn (1970) have indicated, the gap between financial aid income and expenditure is one of the most serious financial problems facing private liberal arts colleges. A number of institutions are being forced to limit expenditures in this area. Wesleyan University, for example, put a ceiling on the unrestricted funds that would be allocated to undergraduate financial aid programs. Unfortunately, such a policy may also result in an increasingly "wasp-waisted" distribution of students—the rich who can afford it and the poor who can get government aid.

Finally, there are savings to be found in auxiliary enterprises. The record growth during the 1960s left many colleges with huge debt service for dormitories. Further, as a condition of receiving loans from lending institutions, colleges had to agree to spend a certain amount each year on maintenance. Consequently, the operation of auxiliary enterprises at many institutions has a large fixed-cost component.

Nonetheless, colleges should constantly reassess their auxiliary operations to determine whether there are possible savings. For instance, several institutions found that they could significantly cut costs in food service and dormitory operations. Some institutions—Adelphi University, for example—have contracted out their food services. Again, one wonders why profit-oriented organizations can do the same task and make a profit, while colleges are unable to manage these operations efficiently.

Conclusion

Private colleges are busy adjusting to the "new depression" in higher education. The recent depressed era found an increasing number of private institutions running deficits. But as traumatic as this recent period has been, it will appear insignificant when compared with the "coming depression," because demographers forecast a significant long-term drop in the student-age population. And the drop will be so large that the current difficulties may pale by comparison. The ability of private colleges to survive hinges on the effectiveness with which their management adapts to this turbulent environment. Survival will depend heavily on good planning and solid management. The increasing emphasis on forward or "strategic" planning is different from the opportunistic program planning that has traditionally dominated academic institutions. In the long run, the financial viability of private colleges depends on developing and maintaining an attractive academic program for a broad spectrum of students.

As the number of students in the traditional college-age cohort begins its precipitous decline around 1983, academic programs will have to become increasingly attractive to a nontraditional clientele. Planning for these students must carefully identify potential student markets. We have noted several cases in which institutions developed innovative academic programs to attract students who otherwise would not have matriculated. Attracting nontraditional students is not impossible, but the task is fraught with the dangers of wishful thinking and overestimation of their willingness to enroll. And the competition from other institutions chasing the same pot of gold is fierce.

Colleges will also continue to serve the traditional college students, even though their numbers will decline. Policies that cause erosion in the quality of faculty, the scope of academic programs, and the condition of physical facilities may help in the short run, but eventually decline in basic quality will undoubtedly pose threats to the ability of some institutions to attract students.

Cutting through all these strategies is a fundamental question: Who should control the decisions about where the colleges are going in the future? As college managers take a stronger lead in curricular planning, a number of issues surrounding governance arise. What should be the role of faculty and students in curricular planning? How is the concept of "shared authority" affected by the lead taken by administrators in curricular planning? What should be the relationships among academic "governance," shared decision processes, and an increasingly sophisticated college "management" system? These questions, coupled with the basic issue of survival, pose a major challenge for colleges facing the economic crisis. Management innovations, such as the ones described and evaluated in this book, are a necessary part but only a small part of the solution.

References

Arcuri, F. W., Mason, T. R., and Meredith, M. "The Impact of Academic Program Structure on the Utilization of Space and Time Resources of Colleges and Universities: A Research Model." In C. B. Johnson and W. G. Katzenmeyer (Eds.), *Management Information Systems in Higher Education: The State of the Art*. Durham, N.C.: Duke University Press, 1969.

Baldridge, J. V. *Power and Conflict in the University*. New York: Wiley, 1971.

Baldridge, J. V., and Deal, T. *Managing Change in Academic Organizations*. Berkeley, Calif.: McCutchan, 1974.

Bogard, L. *Management in Institutions of Higher Education*. Papers on Efficiency in the Management of Higher Education (Technical Report). Berkeley, Calif.: Carnegie Commission on Higher Education, 1972.

Bowen, H. R. "Faculty Salaries: Past and Future." *Educational Record*, Winter 1968, pp. 9-21.

Bowen, H. R., and Douglas, G. L. *Efficiency in Liberal Education*. New York: McGraw-Hill, 1971.

Bowen, H. R., and Minter, W. J. *Private Higher Education: First Annual Report*. Washington, D.C.: Association of American Colleges, 1975.

Bowen, H. R., and Minter, W. J. *Private Higher Education: Second Annual Report*. Washington, D.C.: Association of American Colleges, 1976.

Bowen, W. G. "Economic Pressures on the Major Private Universities." In *The Economics and Financing of Higher Education in the United States: A Compendium of Papers Submitted to the Joint Economics Committee*. Washington, D.C.: Congress of the United States, 1969.

Brady, R. W., and others. *Administrative Data Processing: The Case for Executive Management Involvement*. Boulder, Colo.: National Center for Higher Education Management Systems, Western Interstate Commission for Higher Education, 1975.

Cheit, E. F. *The New Depression in Higher Education*. New York: McGraw-Hill, 1971.

Cheit, E. F. *The New Depression in Higher Education—Two Years Later*. New York: McGraw-Hill, 1973.

Clark, D. G., and others. *Introduction to the Resource Requirements Prediction Model I.G.* Boulder, Colo.: National Center for Higher Education Management Systems, Western Interstate Commission for Higher Education, 1973.

Cohen, M. D., and March, J. G. *Leadership and Ambiguity*. New York: McGraw-Hill, 1974.

Drucker, P. *Practice of Management*. New York: Doubleday, 1954.

Gray, P. *College and University Planning Models*. Paper presented at "Academic Planning for the Eighties and Nineties." Los Angeles: Office of Institutional Studies, University of Southern California, January 22–23, 1976a.

Gray, P. *Faculty Planning Models: The Use of Faculty Simulation Models*. Paper presented at "Academic Planning for the Eighties and Nineties." Los Angeles: Office of Institutional Studies, University of Southern California, January 22–23, 1976b.

Green, E. J. *Effective Planning.* Pittsburgh: Planning Dynamics Company, 1975.

Gwynn, J. "The Data-Based Approach to a Management Information System." In W. J. Minter and B. Lawrence (Eds.), *Management Information Systems: Their Development and Use in the Administration of Higher Education.* Boulder, Colo.: Western Interstate Commission for Higher Education, 1969.

Hopkins, D. S. P. "On the Use of Large-Scale Simulation Models for University Planning." *Review of Educational Research,* 1971, *41* (5), 467–478.

Hussain, K. M., and Freytag, H. L. *Resource, Costing, and Planning Models in Higher Education.* Munich: Verlag Dokumentation, 1973.

Jellema, W. W. *From Red to Black? The Financial Status of Private Colleges and Universities.* San Francisco: Jossey-Bass, 1973.

Jenny, H. H., and Wynn, G. R. *The Golden Years: A Study of Income and Expenditure Growth and Distribution of 48 Private Four-Year Liberal Arts Colleges—1960–1968.* Wooster, Ohio: College of Wooster, 1970.

Judy, R. W. "Systems Analysis for Efficient Resource Allocation in Higher Education: A Report on the Development and Implementation of CAMPUS Techniques." In W. J. Minter and B. Lawrence (Eds.), *Management Information Systems: Their Development and Use in the Administration of Higher Education.* Boulder, Colo.: Western Interstate Commission for Higher Education, 1969.

Katz, D., and Kahn, R. "Organizational Change." In J. V. Baldridge and T. E. Deal (Eds.), *Managing Change in Educational Organizations.* Berkeley, Calif.: McCutchan, 1975.

Kirshling, W. R. "Models: Caveat, Reflections, and Suggestions." In T. R. Mason (Ed.), *New Directions for Institutional Research: Assessing Computer-Based System Models,* no. 9. San Francisco: Jossey-Bass, 1976.

Koenig, H. E. "A Systems Model for Management, Planning, and Resource Allocation in Institutions of Higher Education." In W. J. Minter and B. Lawrence (Eds.), *Management Information Systems: Their Development and Use in the Administra-*

tion of Higher Education. Boulder, Colo.: Western Interstate Commission for Higher Education, 1969,

Levine, J. B. "The Implementation of CAMPUS Simulation Models for University Planning." In W. J. Minter and B. Lawrence (Eds.), *Management Information Systems: Their Development and Use in the Administration of Higher Education*. Boulder, Colo.: Western Interstate Commission for Higher Education, 1969.

Mann, R. L., and others. *An Overview of Two Recent Surveys of Administrative Computer Operations in Higher Education*. Boulder, Colo.: National Center for Higher Education Management Systems, Western Interstate Commission for Higher Education, 1975.

Mason, R. D. "Basic Concepts for Designing Management Information Systems." In A. Rappaport (Ed.), *Information for Decision Making: Quantitative and Behavioral Dimensions*. (2nd ed.) Englewood Cliffs, N.J.: Prentice-Hall, 1975.

Meeth, L. R. *Quality Education for Less Money: A Sourcebook for Improving Cost Effectiveness*. San Francisco: Jossey-Bass, 1974.

Millett, J. D. *Financing Higher Education in the United States*. New York: Columbia University Press, 1952.

Minter, W. J., and Bowen, H. R. *Private Higher Education: Third Annual Report*. Washington, D.C.: Association of American Colleges, 1977.

National Federation of College and University Business Officers Associations. *The Sixty College Study ... A Second Look*. Washington, D.C.: National Federation of College and University Business Officers Associations, 1960.

Newman, F., and others. *Report on Higher Education*. Washington, D.C.: U.S. Government Printing Office, 1971.

Odiorne, G. S. *Management by Objectives*. New York: Pitman, 1965.

Plourde, P. J. "Institutional Use of Models: Hope or Continued Frustration?" In T. R. Mason (Ed.), *New Directions for Institutional Research: Assessing Computer-Based System Models*, no. 9. San Francisco: Jossey-Bass, 1976.

Romney, L. C. *Higher Education Facilities Inventory and Classification Manual*. Boulder, Colo.: National Center for Higher

Education Management Systems, Western Interstate Commission for Higher Education, 1972.

Russell, J. D., and Doi, J. I. *Manual for Studies of Space Utilization in Colleges and Universities*. Athens, Ohio: American Association of Collegiate Registrars and Admissions Officers, 1957.

Schroeder, R. G. "A Survey of Operations Analysis in Higher Education." Paper presented at the 41st national meeting of the Operations Research Society of America, Minneapolis, April 26–28, 1972.

Sonnestein, B. "Long-Range Planning at Wesleyan." *Business Officer*, 1977, *11* (3).

Weathersby, G. B., and Weinstein, M. C. *A Structural Comparison of Analytical Models for University Planning*. Berkeley: Ford Foundation Program for Research In University Administration, 1970.

Index

213

Deans, and political dynamics, 180–182. *See also* Academic officers, chief; Administrators

Decision making: at Arkansas College, 98–99, 103; at Clarkson College of Technology, 72–73; conclusion about, 9; at Earlham College, 115–116; following through on, 178–179; legitimacy of, increased, 154–155; and management information systems, 44; and management by objectives, 85–86; and resource allocation models, 72–73; speed of, and data, 147–149

Degree, completion of, accuracy of information on, 18–21, 22, 23

Delphi technique, at Furman University, 90

Departments: direct costs of, 123–124; enrollment increases by, under management information systems, 157–158; equalized expenditures among, 127–131; and indirect costs, 158–159; interdependency of, 154, 158

Development, directors of, accuracy of information of, 19, 22, 24, 25. *See also* Administrators

Development, effective programs of, 198–199

Doi, J. I., 36

Douglas, G. L., 203

Drake University, 3

Drucker, P., 79

E

Earlham College, xii, xiii, 3; administrative changes at, 116–117; budgeting at, 112–113, 118; consultants at, 112; data base at, 108–109, 118–119; decision making at, 115–116; faculty at, 106, 116; goals at, 109–111; leadership at, 119; long-range planning at, 107–113; participatory planning at, analysis of, 104–120; planning at, 107, 114, 118, 119–120, 152; Resource Requirements Prediction Model

at, 107, 109, 118; staff planning skills at, 111–112; students at, 104–105; success at, 113–117; weaknesses at, 117–119

Educational Testing Service, 90, 116

EDUTRAIN, of Adelphi University, 157, 195–196

Enrollment: continuing, accuracy of information on, 18–20, 22, 23; data on, 147; freshman, accuracy of information on, 18–20, 21, 22, 23; growth in, impact of, 122–123; of nontraditional students, 195–196; projections of, at Clarkson College of Technology, 69–70; total, accuracy of information on, 18–20, 22, 23

Expenditures: administrative, 204–206; deflated, 124, 127; instructional, 11–12, 202–204; pattern of, 200–201; per student, conclusions about, 9–10; reducing, 199–206. *See also* Instructional costs

Exxon Education Foundation, x, xiii, 2–3, 4, 6, 16, 53, 61, 68, 79, 98, 107, 123, 146, 189, 191

F

Faculty: accuracy of information on, 18–20, 22, 23; at Earlham College, 106, 116; flow models for, 36; junior, replacing senior, 202–203; and planning, 152–153; projected need for, at Clarkson College of Technology, 70–71; salary increases low for, 138, 139, 202; sophistication of, increased, 154–155; support of, importance of, to project, 187–188; at Wesleyan University, 58–59, 62–63, 202. *See also* Student/faculty ratio

Federal government, income from, 193–195

Feldman, C., xiii

Financial aid, directors of, accuracy of information of, 19, 20, 22, 23. *See also* Administrators